C000273074

THE CONCISE
ENCYCLOPEDIA OF
MĀORI MYTH
AND LEGEND

A CONCISE ENCYCLOPEDIA OF MĀORI MYTH AND LEGEND

Margaret Orbell

CANTERBURY UNIVERSITY PRESS

First published in 1998 by
CANTERBURY UNIVERSITY PRESS
University of Canterbury
Private Bag 4800
Christchurch
NEW ZEALAND

Copyright © 1998 Margaret Orbell
Copyright © 1998 Canterbury University Press

ISBN 0-908812-56-6

This book is copyright. Except for the purpose of fair review, no part
may be stored or transmitted in any form or by any means,
electronic or mechanical, including recording or storage
in any information retrieval system, without permission in writing
from the publishers. No reproduction may be made,
whether by photocopying or by any other means, unless a licence
has been obtained from the publisher or its agent.

Designed and typeset by Go Ahead Graphics, Christchurch
Printed by SRM Production Services Sdn. Bhd., Malaysia

Introduction

In traditional Māori belief the sky, Rangi, is the first male and the earth, Papa, the first female. In the beginning these two lay embraced, then they were pushed apart by one of their sons, Tāne [Male], to make room for people to live between them. Afterwards Tāne fathered trees, birds, and last of all, human beings.

The history of the world is the history of ancestors [tūpuna]. The traditions vary somewhat, but Tāne's brothers often include Tangaroa, father of sea creatures; Tū, the first warrior; Rongo, father of the kūmara; Haumia, father of fernroot; and Tāwhirimātea, father of the winds. Sometimes there are others as well. In one tradition Tāne has a sister, Wainui [Great waters], the mother and origin of water.

Since humans and other life forms are bound by the indissoluble ties of kinship, Māori did not see their existence as something separate and opposed to the world around them. Birds, fish and plants, along with natural phenomena such as the moon, mist, wind and rocks, were felt to possess a life essentially similar to that of human beings. There was not the sharp distinction between nature and culture that occurs in Western thought.

Between them, the earliest ancestors and their immediate descendants determined the characteristic behaviour [tikanga] of men and women, natural phenomena, and other life forms; they set the pattern for their descendants, who behave now as they did then. Men going fishing on the ocean, for instance, are siding with their creator, Tāne, in his ancient quarrel with Tangaroa, father of the fish – and their waka itself is Tāne, because it is hollowed from a tree, another of Tāne's children.

Succeeding generations, who are exclusively human, become rather more specialised in their activities. Some of these early ancestors satisfy human needs, as when the trickster hero Māui acquires fire, invents spear-points, slows the passage of the sun, and pulls up the fish that becomes Aotea (the North Island).

Further down the genealogies [whakapapa] we come to the men and women who leave their homes in Hawaiki to sail to Aotearoa and become ancestors of the peoples now living in different parts of the country. Traditions telling of such voyages exist in every region.

These ancestors sailed on vessels such as *Te Arawa, Tainui, Tākitimu, Māmari, Horouta* and many more. During the voyage they displayed remarkable powers, overcoming many dangers, and on their arrival they introduced valuable resources such as the kūmara and the karaka tree. They then explored the land, establishing territorial boundaries, placing in the hills and on the shore the mauri – the tapu sources of vitality – that ensured fertility, and creating landmarks. In the south, for instance, Rākaihaitū, captain of the *Uruao*, dug out a number of lakes that the country needed. In the north, the powerful tohunga Ngātoro-i-rangi introduced the volcanic fires still to be found there.

After telling of the voyage to Aotearoa and the definitive acts that occurred subsequently, the traditions of each iwi trace through the genealogies the famous ancestors who founded descent groups, defended their lands against outsiders, avenged defeats, and made politically significant marriages that ensured their people's wellbeing – or, in some cases, stubbornly chose for themselves the person they would marry. These narratives relating to more recent events can generally be described as legends rather than myths, in that they contain much that is historically accurate. A tremendous amount of historical information is available, especially for the last few centuries.

While stories telling of encounters with supernatural beings such as taniwha, fairies [patupaiarehe] and giant reptiles are often set in the distant past, human involvement with them continued. Most taniwha had a relationship with one particular people, who made them offerings; fairies were seen on misty hills and in dreams, and again might have a relationship with humans; even reptiles, in the form of the small geckos that were so dreaded, might be employed in sorcery or made guardians of buried treasure. Traditions relating to such beings were part of a complex body of belief and practice.

This heritage of tradition goes back in its origins to the tropical islands from which the ancestors of the Māori set out to explore the southern ocean, and discovered Aotearoa. In the Cook Islands, Tahiti and Hawai'i, more remotely in Sāmoa and Tonga, there are traditions which are related to Māori ones and can be traced back, in some cases, more than 2,000 years. Nevertheless the Māori traditions, like their culture and society generally, were most distinctively their own.

When Māori people acquired a knowledge of reading and writing, they began at once to make extensive use of it in letters and records of all kinds. From the mid-1840s, tribal authorities in all parts of the country were writing down, or occasionally dictating, mythic narratives, recent histories, accounts of cultural practices and the words of songs of all kinds. They continued to do this throughout the latter part of the nineteenth century and into the early years of the twentieth century.

Sometimes the traditions were recorded and passed down within a family. In many cases, though, such documents resulted from an association between a Māori authority and an interested Pākehā, and most of these records have ended up in public libraries. Some manuscripts have been published in part, others not at all. They now require editing and translation in accord with modern standards, and publication in full.

This vast collection of documents is unusual, when compared to records existing elsewhere, in its sheer size. There must be few if any comparable peoples whose early writings are so prolific. Also, because the first of these records were made very soon after the culture began to change, we have a great deal of information about the functions of these narratives in ritual, songs and oratory, the ways in which their images resonate elsewhere in Māori life and thought.

This book is intended as an introduction to this large and diverse field. It points the way to an ancient tradition which has been preserved both orally and in written form, and is now being rediscovered.

Aituā
Evil Fate

The word aituā means 'disaster, fate'. Often it becomes a personification, so that orators and poets speak of Aituā, or Fate. Who, they ask, can withstand the strong hand of Aituā?

It is something at least to have a person to blame.

Ancestors
Source and substance of the world

Ancestors [tūpuna] were regarded as the substance of their descendants, their very being. This was more than a close bond, it was a continuity of existence.

It was believed that individuals had participated in the lives of their ancestors, so that their own lives went backward in time to early events. An orator describing an early event in his people's history might speak as though he himself had been present at the scene. At the same time, it was thought that people behave as they do because of the presence within them of their ancestors: that they owe their identity to the men and women who have preceded them. These two ideas were inseparable. People were present in their ancestors, and their ancestors were present in them.

The earliest ancestors make up the world (they are the sky, earth, plants and so on), and some are human beings as well. Rangi and Papa are not only sky and earth, they are the first man and woman, and accordingly they establish the basic natures of men and women. Tāne [Male], who gives the world its structure and fathers the birds, plants and humans, provides a further precedent for human males.

The first of the ancestors who follow (men such as Māui, women such as Hine-te-iwaiwa) are, most of them, exclusively human. These people live, it is often said, in Hawaiki. Sometimes they shape and order the world in various ways. Always their activities provide precedents for human circumstances and behaviour.

From these early generations the genealogists trace lines of descent down through the men and women who sailed from Hawaiki to Aotearoa, explored the new land and made it ready for their descendants. When the recital continues to the present, forty or fifty generations may separate a living person from Rangi and Papa.

Relatively recent ancestors had a continuing interest in the behaviour and welfare of their descendants, and watched to ensure that they observed the tapu restrictions necessary for men and women of mana. They might also communicate with relatives in various ways and warn of coming danger.

Aoraki
A man who became a mountain

Aoraki (Mount Cook) is the highest mountain in Aotearoa. A tradition explains that this mountain was once a man, one of the sons of Raki the sky (in the South Island the sky is Raki, rather than Rangi as in the north).

When Raki married Papa, the earth, they already had children from other unions. So Aoraki and his younger brothers came down from the sky to inspect their father's new wife and visit her children. They arrived in an immense waka known as *Te Waka-a-Aoraki* [Aoraki's waka].

They found Papa in the ocean, a huge body of land consisting mostly of Hawaiki; they sailed right around her, then set off to discover other countries. But wherever they went they found only the ocean. So they attempted to return to the sky, but disaster overtook them and the vessel began to sink. As this happened it turned to stone and earth, and it heeled over, leaving the western side much higher than the eastern. The four men climbed to the higher side and turned into mountains; Aoraki is the tallest peak, and his brothers stand nearby.

Some time later a man named Tū-te-rakiwhānoa prepared the land for human habitation. To the north-east the carved prow had fallen and shattered to pieces, forming inlets and islands (known now as the Marlborough Sounds); these he left as they were. But on the east coast he heaped up Horo-maka (Banks Peninsula), and he sent an assistant, Maro-kura, to form the Kaikōura Peninsula. On the south-west coast he chopped out openings with his great adze to let the sea flow into the land.

According to this southern story, the famous Māui who fished up Te Ika a Māui (the North Island) was a descendant of Aoraki. Māui's task was to sail around Aoraki's waka and make it safe for people to land on.

Others say that Aoraki was a member of the crew of *Āraiteuru* who turned to stone along with his companions. And many claim that the entire South Island is Māui's waka.

Aotea

A west coast waka

Turi and his people set sail for Aotearoa because of a war with the great rangatira Uenuku. Although they had won a battle they knew that if they stayed, Uenuku would win in the end.

On board the *Aotea* Turi stowed seed kūmara (under the special care of Rongorongo), seeds of the karaka and other plants, certain birds, and other creatures. His ship brought so many things that it is known proverbially as '*Aotea* utanga rau' [the heavily laden *Aotea*].

The tohunga on board included Tuau and Kauika. As well there was a man named Tapō, who soon behaved insolently towards Turi. Thrown into the ocean, he swam fearlessly after the ship until the people realised that he was under the protection of the god Maru and took him back on board. After this their main god was Maru and his tohunga was Tapō.

During the voyage the *Aotea* put in at an island, Rangitahua, where the vessel was refitted and a dog was sacrificed to Maru with a request for a safe passage. This was granted. But first there was trouble, because of Potoru.

Some say this man came on the *Aotea*, others that he captained the *Ririno*, which accompanied it. Potoru broke tapu in a terrible way by eating the sacrificed dog that belonged to Maru, and as a consequence he went mad. He therefore urged upon Turi a course that nearly led to disaster. Turi had directed the bow of the waka towards the rising sun, but Potoru argued that they should sail instead towards the setting sun. For a while Turi listened, and the ship was caught in strong currents going down into the mouth of Te Parata, the monster at the edge of the ocean. Then when all seemed lost, Turi recited a chant that brought the waka up from the depths. He recited another chant and bailed water from the vessel, then with a third chant he brought the *Aotea* to land, near a harbour known now as the Aotea. He and his crew then set off southwards to find their new home.

At Pātea in southern Taranaki, Turi erected a tūāhu and built a pā and a house of learning. On land nearby, his wife Rongorongo planted the eight kūmara she had brought from Hawaiki – and when autumn came, they harvested 800 basketsful.

After Turi's death, dissension arose when his daughter Tāne-roroa, having married a man named Uenga-puanake, became pregnant and craved dog meat. Her husband killed and cooked a dog belonging to her brother, Tūranga-i-mua, and the theft was discovered. So Tāne-roroa and her husband crossed the river and lived on the north bank, where their son Ruanui became the founding ancestor of the people of Ngāti Ruanui. The descendants of the sons of Turi and Rongorongo continued to live on the south bank and became known as Ngā Rauru.

Descent from *Aotea* is claimed as well by many peoples to the south, among them those in the Whanganui and Rangitīkei regions.

Aotearoa
Traditionally, the North Island

In earlier times one of the names given the North Island was Aotea. Since this name can be understood as meaning 'white, or clear,' 'cloud, or day,' in a general way it must have been felt to be propitious. Aotearoa, or 'Long Aotea', is a related name for the North Island which has been in use since the nineteenth century, and perhaps before this in some regions.

The name Aotearoa is sometimes explained as meaning 'Land of the long white cloud' and is said to have had its origin in the voyage of the explorer Kupe, when he and his wife Hine-te-apa-rangi glimpsed clouds resting upon high hills in the distance and realised that they had discovered a new land. This tradition was known to some peoples, though not all. It evolved as a way of explaining the meaning of a name already in existence.

In the twentieth century the name Aotearoa came to refer, often, to the entire country, south as well as north. (It is used in this way in this book.) In this sense Aotearoa sometimes refers to the land as it was before the arrival of Pākehā, but increasingly it is employed as a present-day alternative to the name New Zealand. This usage is certain to become increasingly popular.

Apakura
The woman who urged revenge

When someone was killed, it was the duty of the male relatives to obtain revenge. The women's role was to lament the dead and incite the men to undertake this task.

The main mythical figure who set the pattern for women in this respect was Apakura. The murdered man is nearly always Tū-whakararo, her husband (or sometimes eldest son). Usually he has been treacherously slain by Apakura's own brothers. Forced to choose between her own kin and her husband (or son), Apakura very properly seeks revenge for this crime. She weeps constantly, singing her lament, as she seeks out her youngest son, Whakatau. She appeals to him to avenge the death of Tū-whakararo, and he does so.

Apanui-waipapa
Ancestor of Te Whānau-ā-Apanui

Te Whānau-ā-Apanui, a people whose lands on the East Coast extend from a point north of Tōrere to a landmark east of Cape Runaway, take their name from Apanui-waipapa. This man lived at Whāngārā with his eight children. He was killed by his uncle Hauiti, but his children escaped to Maraenui, at the mouth of the Mōtū River.

According to one account Hauiti followed them there, but an Arawa relative, Turirangi, came to their assistance and killed Hauiti. The young men were so grateful that they gave Turirangi their sister, Rongomai-hua-tahi. From this union came Apanui-ringa-mutu, whose son was Tūkākī. He in turn had three notable sons, Te Ehutu, Kaiaio and Tamahae.

Āraiteuru
A taniwha at Hokianga

This female taniwha is sometimes said to have arrived from the homeland of Hawaiki before the *Māmari*, and sometimes to have escorted this waka during its voyage.

Āraiteuru was pregnant when she arrived, and soon gave birth to eleven sons. Each set out on a journey of exploration, digging a trench with his nose as he went, and together they created the many branches of the Hokianga Harbour.

Āraiteuru lives in a cave on the south head of the Hokianga Harbour, where heavy surf breaks across the bar. She is a guardian of the region, but in former times she might also, when angry, raise storms and wreck vessels on the bar. A companion, a taniwha often known as Niwa, lives by the north head of the harbour.

Āraiteuru
A petrified cargo and crew

The *Āraiteuru* arrived from Hawaiki and made its way southwards. Its entire crew turned into mountains, hills, and pillars of rock.

As the waka sailed down the east coast of the South Island, several of the crew plunged into the sea, swam ashore and became mountains. A storm swept the ship on as far as Matakaea (Shag Point), where it was wrecked; it turned into a reef along with the captain, Hipo. The cargo was swept ashore at Moeraki, where large numbers of spherical and elongated boulders are the petrified eel pots, gourds and kūmara the vessel was carrying.

When the crew struggled ashore they were very cold, so they set out that same night to look for firewood. They had many adventures, then when day came they turned to stone. More than 150 mountains and ranges were believed to have had their origin in this event.

Atua
Unseen powers

This word atua can be translated as 'god' or 'spirit,' although there was no worship of atua, no ceremonies just to praise them. Māori had contact with their atua and made them offerings on occasions such as the presentation of first-fruits, and when there was a specific need for communication and assistance.

Every family of rank had a relationship with the wairua [souls] of recent ancestors, who visited them as atua. Offerings were made to these atua. Sometimes a small basket of food would be hung from a tree near the tapu grove that held the body of a deceased relative; if a small bird ate this food it was known that the spirit had accepted the offering and would help his or her descendants.

Since persons of mana had inherited this quality from ancestors, their ancestral spirits watched to ensure that they respected the tapu restrictions that accompanied this high status. If they broke the rules of tapu, even accidentally, the spirits might punish them with illness.

For large issues, especially success in war, there were also the atua who had been brought from Hawaiki: Uenuku, Maru, Kahukura and many others. Offerings were made to small figures of these gods, or other objects representing them.

Atua kahukahu
Malignant spirits

The wairua of aborted foetuses and stillborn children were potentially ill-disposed towards the living; having never known their relatives they owed them no loyalty, and they might resent the fact that they had been deprived of life. To prevent such a wairua from afflicting people with illness and perhaps killing them, it was necessary to bury the body with appropriate rituals. Occasionally this was not done, or the ceremony was not successful, and the wairua turned into a dangerous atua kahukahu.

Atutahi
The first-born star

This is Canopus, second brightest of the visible stars. When Tāne, creating the world, was about to throw his basket of stars into the sky, Atutahi clung to the outside of the basket so that he would be the first-born and could therefore, because of the tapu of high rank, stay aloof from the common horde. The basket of stars became Te Mangō-roa (the Milky Way) and Atutahi still hangs outside, remaining apart.

Being the first-born, and so bright, he is the lord [ariki] of the stars of the year.

Awa-nui-ā-rangi
Son of a celestial father

Two distant but related peoples, Ngāti Awa in the southern Bay of Plenty and Te Āti Awa in northern Taranaki, trace their origins to an ancestor, Awa-nui-ā-rangi, whose father came down from the sky.

In the Bay of Plenty story, a girl was sent to draw water from a stream. As she stooped to fill her gourd, a blaze of light shone around her. She could see nobody, but the shadow of a man fell upon the water. She felt his arms about her, and he told her, 'If you have a boy, name him after the great river [awa nui] of light on which I came down to you.'

This was how Awa-nui-ā-rangi [Great river of sky] received his name. His celestial father is sometimes said to be Tamarau, sometimes Tama-i-waho or even Rangi himself. His mother is often Te Kura, and her earthly husband the famous Toi.

In Taranaki, Awa-nui-ā-rangi's father is Tamarau-te-heketanga-ā-rangi [Tamarau who came down from the sky]. Again the boy is associated with Toi, often as his grandson. This time, a woman named Rongoueroa (or Rongouaroa) went to a stream to wash her son, and found Tamarau behind her. Again she was told to call her child after the 'awa nui' that had brought her lover to the earth; although in this case the 'awa nui' was a powerful [nui] chant of the kind known as an awa.

Birds
Winged children of Tāne

The early ancestor Tāne [Male] is usually regarded as the creator of birds, along with other life forms belonging to the land. In some accounts he goes searching for a human female, and instead meets other kinds of women; he couples with them, and they produce the different kinds of birds. He then creates the trees and other plants, providing birds with their food and their homes.

Since there was believed to be a continuity of existence between ancestors and their descendants, birds could be individually and collectively spoken of as Tāne; they are the form that he takes. But the myths vary. Sometimes the origin of forest birds is Punaweko, and that of seabirds is Hurumanu. Small birds are said by some to owe their origin to Tāne-te-hokahoka.

Most kinds of birds had a particular character assigned to them. The pigeon is quiet and peaceful, the kākā clamorous and active, and individuals might be likened to either bird. Rangatira could be spoken of as harrier hawks because of this bird's association with victory in battle.

Birth
Entrance to the world

Ceremonial feasting and much rejoicing greeted the news that a woman of rank was pregnant, especially when she was expecting her first child. Before the baby's birth a small temporary house was built for the mother, since the rules of tapu did not allow a birth to occur inside a permanent building. She lived there with an attendant, in a tapu state, until the time came for the baby to be born. Relatives were usually with her during the birth. Women gave birth in a kneeling position, often with an attendant facing them.

Childbirth and everything connected with it were under the care of Hine-te-iwaiwa and Hine-kōrako. When Hine-te-iwaiwa, in the beginning, experienced a difficult birth, a ritual chant hastened her son's arrival. Since that time this chant has often been recited to assist a woman in this situation.

The term for the placenta is whenua, a word that also means 'land'. The whenua was taken by the mother or a close relative to a secret place already chosen and ready to receive it, and was buried there. In this way the land that had sustained the child within the woman was brought together with the land that sustains people during their lives. The umbilical cord was also disposed of carefully. It might be placed in a tapu hollow tree or else buried, perhaps at the foot of a boundary post to show the child's claim to this land.

After a baby's cord has been tied and severed, it takes seven or eight days for the end of the cord to fall away. When this final separation from the cord had taken place, a ceremony known as the tohi [separation] ritual was performed by a tohunga to mark the child's entry to this world and proclaim his or her identity.

The conception of a child, and its growth within the mother, was a re-enactment of the occasion when the creator Tāne had made the first human from the soil of Hawaiki. Every man who fathered a child was repeating Tāne's action, forming the child in the homeland of Hawaiki. And the mother's womb, by implication at least, was identified with the soil of Hawaiki.

Death
The soul's journey

Death, like birth, was a transition that could not take place inside a house if people were to continue living there. When a person of rank became ill, a temporary shelter would be erected for them. At the approach of death the person might speak and sing a farewell, giving advice for the future. The rituals performed at the funeral [tangihanga] varied from one region to another, as did the treatment of the body afterwards. The person would sit or lie in state surrounded by weeping relatives while parties of mourners arrived, wept, addressed the person, and sang their farewells.

Laments for the dead [waiata tangi] are among the highest achievements of the great Māori poetic tradition. These songs mourn and praise the person who has died, sending the wairua on the journey it now must make. Usually the wairua was thought to travel to Te Rēinga in the Far North.

After a year or two, when the body had decomposed, the bones were prepared with solemn ritual for their final resting place. Usually the bones of relatives lay together through the generations, often in a hidden cave, sometimes in a hollow tree or other repository. People who had died lived on in their descendants. As well, their wairua continued in many cases to guide and advise them.

A woman, Hine-nui-te-pō [Great woman the night], was held mainly responsible for the existence of death (although there was also the evil Whiro). This is because women have the power to give birth, and the introduction of new life implies that death must follow.

Dogs
Close companions

Dogs were employed when hunting kiwi, kākāpō and takahē, they were the pets of rangatira, cloaks made from their skins were greatly prized, they were favourite items at feasts, and they were offered to the gods at rituals marking major events. Since people and dogs lived closely together (and dogs, apart from humans, were the only land mammals other than bats and the introduced rats), it is not surprising that tradition accords dogs a special status. The first dog's body was formed from the body of a man, Irawaru, and when dog's die they go to the underworld just as humans do, though by a different path.

In myth, an ancestor's dog could be transformed into a rock or cliff – which was still to be seen and bore witness, therefore, to the truth of the story. Such rocks remained dogs, and could be dangerous.

Earth
The mother

The earth is female, as the sky is male, and while the sky is sacred [tapu], the earth in general is everyday, ordinary, profane [noa]. She has to be, because this is where life goes on. Fertility and decay, life, death and more life are what the earth produces. And since people are part of the world, there is no essential difference between the fertility of the earth and that of human women.

The earth was understood in terms of human experience, and the experiences and roles of women were understood in terms of the earth. So the first woman, Papa, was the earth. When Tāne decided to make a wife from the sand of Hawaiki, he went, it is often said, to 'the sands at Kurawaka' [te one i Kurawaka] – and this place is the mons veneris of Papa herself. So while it was Tāne who created Hine-ahu-one, he achieved this by going to the source of Papa's fertility. Hawaiki, as the source of life, is necessarily associated with Papa's life-giving powers.

Later came Hine-nui-te-pō [Great woman the night], who brought death into the world. Inevitably the main responsibility for death is assigned in tradition to women, since life implies eventual death, and they give life. And again the earth comes into this, because Hine-nui-te-pō belongs with Night [Te Pō], which is part of the earth, or perhaps beneath it. Yet the role of Hine-nui-te-pō is complex and may be differently interpreted; she does care for her descendants at the ends of their lives. And while Papa has hidden within her the Night and those who are now down there, new life keeps coming from the earth and from human women.

Fairies
Spirit people

Handsome, uncanny people, known usually as patupaiarehe or tūrehu [fairies], lived on hilltops and other remote places. Their houses and på were built from swirling mist, and they themselves were glimpsed on misty days. Most of the time they were visible only to people with visionary powers [matakite], though others could hear them.

Fairies were atua, but not the usual kind, because they possessed bodies, whereas most atua were bodiless. Like humans the fairies hunted and fished, wove garments, sang, danced and made love, but there were differences. Their skins were pale and their hair was light in colour. Being atua they were highly tapu, so they ate only raw food; they greatly feared cooked food, steam from ovens, fire, even ashes.

Most of the stories about fairies tell how they sought humans as lovers.

The men were expert flute players, and the sound of their music attracted human women. Sometimes a fairy and a human would meet in the forest, or a fairy would visit a human in a house at night. Erotic dreams could be explained in this way, and a further proof was the occasional birth of an albino child, whose pale skin, fair hair, and inability to stand the sunlight were obviously inherited from a fairy father.

Sometimes the fairies support the human order to some extent, even punishing those who break tapu restrictions. In some regions, generations of tohunga had a long-established relationship with the fairies on their people's mountain. But generally the fairies were believed to have been living in the land before the arrival of the first humans, and to have been displaced by them. There was a feeling that the products of the land really belonged to them, and placatory offerings might be made by fishermen or men digging fernroot.

In many places humans were thought to have gained a knowledge of plaiting and weaving techniques from the fairies, usually by tricking them into continuing their work until the sun rose, so that they fled the light and left behind their nets or weaving.

Fernroot
A reliable food

Fernroot is not a root but the rhizome of the bracken fern. In good soil this plant grows to three metres in height and has starchy rhizomes up to forty-five centimetres in length. Such plants were productive and needed almost no attention, while dried fernroot would keep for years. So though fernroot was liked much less than kūmara, it was a staple food in many areas.

Before use the dried rhizomes were soaked in water, roasted in embers, scraped, then pounded with a wooden mallet. Only the starchy part was eaten, the fibres being rejected. Often there was a relish of dried fish or shellfish.

Fernroot was proverbially reliable as a source of food. Perhaps because of this, and because it was firmly rooted and considered a strengthening food, it was believed that a small piece of fernroot worn around the neck would protect the wearer from minor afflictions such as headaches. And since fernroot was regarded as a food suitable for warriors and others engaged in arduous pursuits, it was often associated with warfare. In ritual it was opposed to the kūmara, which belonged with peace and festivity. The parent of fernroot is generally Haumia.

Fish
Tangaroa's children

The early ancestor Tangaroa, whose realm is the sea, is the parent of fish and other sea creatures. In some traditions, however, certain fish are assigned other parents, as when sharks, with whales and other marine mammals, are children of Punga.

Orators and poets spoke of fish and other sea creatures as possessing distinctive qualities. Whales, especially sperm whales, were thought to be like rangatira, so high-ranking men could be likened to them. As well, whales were associated with rich food and abundance, since those stranded on the shore presented their finders with enormous quantities of meat and oil.

Warriors could be compared to sharks, also to the little yellow-eyed mullet that leap so vigorously. Other creatures had more specialised roles in metaphor. In inland waters, some species of kōkopu have beautiful markings, so an admired object might be described as 'mottled like a kōkopu'.

More generally, fish in Māori symbolic thought have the special role of being caught and put to use; this was the very reason for their existence. Because of this, people who had been defeated in warfare were frequently spoken of as fish. The land itself had been a fish, brought up from the depths by Māui and made a home for human beings. The much-treasured greenstone was another resource that had been a fish – and had swum all the way from Hawaiki, followed by its owner Ngahue.

Gourds
A treasured plant

Some young gourds were eaten as vegetables and the rest were left to mature for use as containers. They were trained into the shapes required, their contents were removed, and they were dried and hardened in the sun and beside fires. Pū-tē-hue is in some regions the parent of the gourd. An East Coast belief is that a man named Māia introduced gourds from Hawaiki.

In the far south, where gourds would not grow, containers for water and preserved birds were made from bull kelp, which flourishes on the coast there.

Greenstone
Ngahue's fish

Greenstone, or jade, was obtainable only in the South Island, in remote, rugged places on the west coast and to a lesser extent in Fiordland and Central Otago. Being extremely hard and tough it was very difficult to work, until a new technique of abrasive cutting was developed some five hundred years ago. This was most laborious but gave workmen precise control over their materials. From that time greenstone adzes and chisels were used extensively in woodworking, and finer carving became possible. Pieces of greenstone were the most precious of trade commodities, passed from hand to hand until they reached the most distant parts of the country.

Greenstone was treasured for its beauty, hardness and indestructibility. Pendants that had been worn by departed relatives were venerated because of their associations with the dead, and kinsfolk wept over them and sang laments.

Several myths explain the origin of greenstone. In one of the best known, greenstone was a fish named Poutini that swam from Hawaiki to its present location in Aotearoa. This fish was the pet of a man named Ngahue.

Hakawau
A tohunga who fought evil

When Hakawau was young and knew no magic, a girl he loved, named Rona, was kidnapped by atua at the command of Pāka, an old sorcerer who lived on the Rangitoto Range. Knowing that Pāka could be conquered only through ritual powers, Hakawau left his home at Kāwhia and travelled to the Urewera Mountains to learn chants from his uncle, a powerful tohunga. On his return he set out for Pāka's home with a few chosen warriors.

Outside Pāka's pā Hakawau could see, though his companions could not, Pāka's atua waiting to destroy them. He sent out his own army of spirits, and they overcame Pāka's spirits. At once the mana of Rangitoto was gone. Hakawau restored Rona to her relatives, and soon afterwards she married him.

On another occasion Hakawau overcame two sorcerers, Puarata and Tautohito, whose pā was at Puketapu, near the south head of the Manukau Harbour. These men possessed a carved head with terrible powers, a vessel for powerful atua. When travellers approached, these spirits would inform the head and it would shout with a voice so loud that the strangers would perish. Soon the bones of many men lay on that path, and people living in distant places knew of the head and dreaded it.

Hakawau resolved to test the strength of this head. With a single servant he made his way northwards from Kāwhia, repeating chants to ward off the attacks of enemy atua. After crossing the Waikato River they passed the bodies of those the head had destroyed, and they expected death at every moment. But they continued on, and when Hakawau came within sight of the enemy pā he sent his atua forward to attack those of the enemy. The spirits on both sides engaged in battle, and Hakawau's spirits were triumphant.

Hākirirangi
A skilled horticulturalist

In the Tūranga (Gisborne) district, this woman is usually said to have come from Hawaiki on the *Tākitimu*, bringing with her a basket containing seed kūmara. At Tūranga she planted her kūmara, and established the proper procedures for growing them. She worked diligently, and her plants yielded heavy crops.

Some people in the region associate Hākirirangi with the *Horouta* rather than the *Tākitimu*, and some call her Hine-hākirirangi. All agree in honouring her as the person who brought the kūmara and showed how it should be grown.

Hākuturi
Guardians of the forest

It was the task of the Multitude of the Hākuturi [te Tini o te Hākuturi] to protect the forests in Hawaiki and avenge any desecration of their tapu. When Rata felled a tree without performing the proper ritual, the Hākuturi punished him by making the tree stand upright again. Afterwards, however, they adzed the tree into a waka for him, completing their work in a single night.

These forest guardians seem generally to have been regarded as birds. One writer calls them the children of Tāne.

Hani and Puna
Sacred stones at Kāwhia

The final resting-place of the *Tainui*, after its voyage from Hawaiki, was near Maketū on the Kāwhia Harbour. The waka lies under the soil, turned to stone, and two limestone pillars mark the positions of the prow and stern. Some say these tapu pillars are themselves the prow and sternpost, others that they were placed there by the ship's captain, Hoturoa, and the tohunga, Raka-taura.

Raka-taura's pillar is the prow, which stands at the higher, inland end of the waka. Its name is Hani, or Hani-whakarere-tāngata [Hani who destroys people], and its power is that of the warrior spirit. Hoturoa's stone on the seaward side is the sternpost Puna, or Puna-whakatupu-tāngata [Spring that makes people increase]. This has the power of fertility, including the ability to create human beings.

In a different account, drawn from the esoteric lore of the Tainui peoples as it existed in the late nineteenth century and subsequently, Hani is the male essence and Puna the female essence. In the beginning these two were apart, and they sought constantly to unite. They passed separately through the Bespaced Heavens, then merged at last in the high god Io. Until this time, Io was not fully evolved. When male and female entered him, he assumed his final form; and he has within him, therefore, the powers of both male and female.

Hape
An early inhabitant

Some trace Hape's ancestry to Toi, who was here in the beginning, and others to Māui himself, who fished up the land. Other accounts have him arriving from Hawaiki on the *Rangi-mātoru*, bringing the kūmara. It is agreed that he was the founding ancestor of a people known, because of their early origin, as Te Hapū Oneone [The people of the soil]. These people belong mostly to Ōhiwa and the Waimana and Rūātoki valleys.

Hape is sometimes said to have come from Hawaiki in search of greenstone. After living for a while at Ōhiwa he set off on a long journey to Te Wai Pounamu (the South Island). There he found greenstone, and there he finally died.

Back at Ōhiwa, Hape's sons Rawaho and Tamarau had discovered that their kūmara crops no longer flourished, because their father had taken with him the mauri that held the mana of the kūmara. So the brothers set off in pursuit. After many adventures they found themselves in Te Wai Pounamu, standing before the tapu house where their father lay dead.

The story now becomes an account of the rivalry between these two. Rawaho was the elder, and he was a tohunga. But now, as he recited lengthy chants before entering the house, he waited too long. His younger brother recited shorter chants and entered first.

Inside, Tamarau found Hape's desiccated body. Following an ancient ritual, he closed his teeth upon Hape's ear and at once inherited his father's powers. He was now an atua. He possessed himself of the two belts that contained the mauri of the kūmara, and informed his elder brother that it was too late for him to inherit their father's powers.

Back at Ōhiwa Tamarau showed kindness towards Rawaho, presenting him with the mauri of the kūmara so that his crops did well. Tamarau became the atua of his descendants and protected them in times of war.

A different story about Hape is told by the Arawa peoples. They say that their early ancestor Ngātoro-i-rangi confronted Hape at Taupō while both were travelling separately through the region. Ngātoro-i-rangi suspected that Hape was there to claim land for himself and his descendants, so to assert his own claim he began the ascent of Ngāuruhoe. Seeing Hape climbing up behind him, he called upon his gods to destroy his rival. They sent sleet and snow, and Hape perished.

Hāpōpō
Always a loser

Hāpōpō is a minor figure who turns up in several myths. Always he trusts to appearances and is deceived.

In a Ngāti Porou story, Hāpōpō is an ally of Wheta, enemy of the great Uenuku and his son Whatiua. Under cover of darkness, a party of men led by Whatiua surround Wheta's house. These warriors hear

Hāpōpō, inside, anxiously asking his atua whether the enemy are on their way. The god reassures Hāpōpō that he is entirely safe, that no attack will come. But soon afterwards Hāpōpō, with others, is attacked and killed.

Hatupatu
An Arawa hero

After arriving from Hawaiki on *Te Arawa*, Hatupatu settled with his relatives on Mokoia Island in Lake Rotorua. He was the youngest son, and his three brothers treated him badly.

On a bird-hunting expedition into the interior, two of the brothers, Hānui and Hāroa, ate the good birds themselves and gave Hatupatu the tough ones. In the end, the boy planned mischief. In his brothers' absence he ate up the birds they had preserved in gourds and bark containers, then he disturbed everything in the camp to make it seem the work of a visiting war party. After this he wounded himself in a couple of places and lay covered in blood.

Hatupatu's brothers believed his story. But when he kept stealing the potted birds they caught him in the act, killed him, and buried him in the heap of feathers plucked from their birds. Then they went home and told their parents they did not know what had happened to him. The parents, suspecting murder, sent out an atua in the form of a blowfly. The spirit found the place where Hatupatu lay buried, and brought him back to life.

So Hatupatu went on through the forest, and he came across a giant woman in the form of a bird, with wings and beak, who was spearing birds for herself. This woman, Kurangaituku, imprisoned him in her cave. But he escaped, taking her fine cloaks, and ran towards his home on Mokoia.

She followed, but he recited a chant and hid inside a rock, then went on again. By the time he reached the hot springs at Whakarewarewa, she was once more close behind. Knowing the springs to be dangerous, Hatupatu jumped right across. Kurangaituku tried to wade through and she was burnt to death.

Hatupatu then dived into Lake Rotorua and swam underwater to his island home. When his brothers learnt of his presence and came to fight him, they found he was no longer a boy but a fearsome warrior. He overcame his brothers and allowed them to live.

Their father then addressed the defeated brothers, telling them that instead of this disgraceful behaviour they should be seeking revenge for the destruction of their ancestral waka, *Te Arawa*. After its voyage from Hawaiki the vessel had been beached at Maketū, and there it had been burnt by Raumati, an enemy from Tauranga.

Shamed by this reproach, the brothers prepared for war. When they set sail, Hatupatu remained behind, then later dived into the lake, taking with him thirty red feather cloaks; after swimming underwater he went on by land. The brothers and their army, reaching their camp that evening, found Hatupatu there ahead of them. Next day the same thing happened; Hatupatu again reached their destination first.

At Maketū the jealous brothers did not place any men under Hatupatu's command, and because of this insult he went off to sleep on his own among some bushes. Then he had an idea. He tied the bushes into bundles and draped his fine cloaks around them, making them look like a band of warriors.

At dawn the rangatira in the brothers' camp rose to encourage their men with warlike speeches, while their hidden enemies watched. When all had finished, Hatupatu rose and addressed his bundles. He made many speeches, each time dressing differently, so it seemed that this division was led by many valorous rangatira. Soon the other side dreaded Hatupatu and his bushes more than his brothers' divisions.

When battle commenced, the cowardly brothers and their men soon ran away, but Hatupatu fought and killed two important rangatira, one of them Raumati himself. Seeing their leaders fall, the enemy turned and fled.

Back at Rotorua, Hatupatu revealed to his father that it was he who had killed Raumati and avenged the burning of *Te Arawa*. From this time on, his rank and mana were greater than those of his brothers.

Near Ātiamuri, a rock beside the road is said to be the one inside which Hatupatu hid from Kurangaituku. This rock is a tipua, a tapu entity with special powers. Offerings of fern and green twigs are still made to it.

Hau
Breath, wind, life

In traditional belief there are in a person's body two presences, a wairua and a hau, that can both be described as souls. The wairua leaves the body during sleep and also after death, though it continues to exist. The hau is always present in the living body, then disappears at death.

This word hau is the usual term for breath, but since breath is life, it has as well a more general significance. Furthermore, it was believed by extension that a hau was possessed by an entire people, and by such valued possessions and resources as a pā, a house, a forest, the ocean. In each case, the life and vitality (the hau) of the entity concerned was preserved and protected by being ritually located within a mauri (a highly tapu object hidden from enemies).

As well, hau is the standard term for wind. Again there was the concept of a living force; the wind was the counterpart of a human's breath.

Hau and Wairaka
A runaway wife

Soon after his arrival from Hawaiki, the early ancestor Hau set out to find his wife Wairaka, who had been abducted by two slaves, Kiwi and Weka. Travelling south from Whanganui he crossed many rivers, and named each of them according to an experience he had there. For instance, finding a large river he feared he could not cross, he called it Manawatū [Nervous-heart].

On the coast by Pukerua Bay, Hau found Wairaka and killed her two companions. He ordered his wife into the sea to collect shellfish, then with a chant he turned her to stone. (She is still there now, a large rock accessible at low tide.) Afterwards Hau continued his journey of exploration as far as Lake Wairarapa.

Hau's full name is Hau-pipi. Generally he is believed to have arrived on the *Aotea*. The Whanganui and Rangitīkei peoples often trace descent from him, and his story provides explanations for the names of rivers and other landmarks.

Hauāuru
The strong west wind

At Tāmaki (Auckland) the west wind, Hauāuru, once coveted Wairaka, the wife of Tamatea-te-rā, who lived in the volcanic peaks in the region. In Tamatea's absence he played soft tunes in the forest trees, winning Wairaka with his music, then took her south with him.

Tamatea traced his wife at last to Arahura, the greenstone valley in Te Wai Pounamu (the South Island); she was sitting by the water while Hauāuru was away searching for greenstone. Tamatea told her to collect shellfish for his dinner, but she knew her infidelity would be punished and she chose to drown. She is now a rock known as Wairaka that stands off the coast near Westport.

Haumapūhia
Creator of Lake Waikaremoana

Haumapūhia was the daughter (some say son) of Māhu, who lived long ago in the Urewera Mountains. One day he told her to draw water from a spring, she refused to go, and in a rage he thrust her under the water. Instead of drowning she turned into a taniwha.

Struggling to escape, she formed the great arms of Lake Waikaremoana. Then she heard the sea far to the south, and attempted to reach it. She forced her way down, forming the underground channel that is the only outlet from the lake, but as she came back up she was overtaken by daylight and turned to stone. She still lies there now, face down in the rushing waters.

Haumia
Origin of fernroot

Fernroot, the starchy rhizome of the bracken fern, was dug in early summer then dried and stored for the winter. Though not liked as much as kūmara, it was valued for the relative ease with which it could be obtained and stored.

Usually it is Haumia who is the fernroot, or father of the fernroot. The Arawa peoples regarded him as one of the sons of Rangi and Papa, the first parents, saying that when these sons fought among themselves in the beginning, Haumia was attacked with others by his brother Tāwhiri-mātea, the wind. He tried to hide in the ground, but his hair stuck out, and he was found and devoured by the warrior Tū (who here repre-sents human beings). Ever since, human beings have eaten their relative Haumia.

In the southern Bay of Plenty and parts of the East Coast, Haumia is a son of Tāne and grandson of Rangi and Papa.

Haumia
A taniwha at Manukau

This taniwha was a powerful atua of the Waikato peoples and regularly communicated with tohunga who were his mediums. His home was in the Manukau Harbour.

On one occasion Haumia informed his tohunga that Ureia, the taniwha of the neighbouring Hauraki peoples, must be killed, and that he himself would entice Ureia to the Manukau. So he visited Ureia, then suggested a return visit: a feast had been prepared, he said, and there were gifts as well. Ureia accepted the invitation.

At Manukau, Haumia's people had placed an enormous noose across the entrance to the harbour and great numbers of men stood ready to pull on the ropes. As the tohunga at the tūāhu recited their chants, Haumia led Ureia straight into the snare. Ureia fought hard but at last was overcome.

This treachery did not go unrevenged. Armies from Hauraki attacked the peoples of Tāmaki, Manukau and Waikato, and some were driven from their homes.

Haumia-whakatere-taniwha
A courageous confrontation

At Kāwhia many generations ago, a man named Haumia owned a kūmara planation on a cliff overlooking the sea. Year after year his crops were destroyed by extraordinarily high waves that reared right up over the cliff. In the end he climbed down the cliff and discovered an immense taniwha living in a cave. This taniwha, whose name was Rapanui, had sent the waves that caused the damage.

Haumia bravely overcame Rapanui and was henceforth known as Haumia-whakatere-taniwha [Haumia who makes taniwha swim away].

Hautapu
A meeting with a fairy

Hunting takahē with his dog on the heights of Mount Tākitimu in the south, Hautapu met a beautiful woman named Kaiheraki. When asked about her people, she said she had no relatives. Her mother was the mountain on which she lived.

Hautapu realised then that she was a fairy [patupaiarehe], and that if he took her as his wife she might keep him there for ever. But he knew the rituals by which this danger could be averted. A sacred fire had to be kindled, and a small portion of food cooked in a special oven. This would destroy Kaiheraki's tapu and make it safe to marry her.

The ritual kindling of fire required the presence of a man and a woman; while the man twirled the upper part of the fire-plough, the woman held the lower part steady with her foot. So Hautapu now showed Kaiheraki what to do. He turned his stick in the groove, the dust began to smoke, and soon there was a little flame. The woman cried out in fear, being unused to fire. Then a spark fell on her foot and it started to bleed, because this is what fire does to these people.

She ran, he caught her, and again they began to make fire. Then his attention was diverted and she fled into the forest. The mist came down and he knew he would never find her.

Kaiheraki is still on her mountain, and on misty days her giant figure can be seen striding along the ridges.

Hawaiki
The homeland in the east

This mythical land is best known as the country from which, in numerous traditions, the ancestors of the different peoples make the voyage to Aotearoa. Sometimes the crew of a waka set out because there has been fighting, or there will be if they stay; generally they have quarrelled with the great rangatira Uenuku, who always wins in the end. In other accounts no motivation is given, or needed.

Nearly all the peoples of Aotearoa have a tradition of such a voyage, or an ancestor who came by other means, perhaps riding on a piece of pumice or on the back of a whale. Even when a people trace descent to an ancestor who was in the country in the beginning (such as Māui or Toi), they often celebrate as well their descent from ancestors who arrived from Hawaiki.

These accounts of astonishing voyages – great dangers overcome through the power of ritual chant, struggles for supremacy between rangatira and tohunga, vessels that subsequently turn to stone, journeys undertaken by leading men to establish landmarks and claim territory in the new land – can be recognised as myths when they are considered in the context of other beliefs about Hawaiki.

Since the sun rises in the east, and so do the stars that bring the seasons with their food resources, this direction was associated in Māori thought with life, fertility and success. Because of this association, Hawaiki was generally said to lie in the direction of the rising sun.

In the beginning, human life itself was created in Hawaiki, because the first human being (it is often said) was shaped from the soil of Hawaiki by Tāne. Many other mythic events occur there, and it is the source of many valued resources.

When the ancestors arrived in their waka, they brought with them treasured plants and birds, important atua, and ritual objects such as mauri. In one way and another, Hawaiki was the ultimate source of the mana of all of these. The crops flourished, the gods exerted their powers, the mauri ensured the continuing fertility of the resources they protected, because of their origin in Hawaiki.

It was often thought that after death some wairua were able to return to the homeland of Hawaiki. At East Cape, this journey was believed to be made in an eastward direction. In other regions an orator at a funeral might tell the deceased person to travel north, or to follow the setting sun to Hawaiki (since the west was associated on such occasions with loss and death).

Hawaiki-rangi
The house with four doors

In the southernmost regions of the North Island, there was a belief that after death a person's wairua often makes its way to Te Hono-i-wairua [The meeting of wairua], in the far land of Irihia. There, it was sometimes said, the wairua enters a house, Hawaiki-rangi [Sky Hawaiki], which stands on the summit of a mountain. Its four doors face east, west, south, and north.

According to a Whanganui poet of the early eighteenth century, three of these doors lead down to Night. This is the destination of many wairua. But the fourth door leads upwards to the sky. In the earliest times the great Tāne passed through that door, climbed up, and reached the highest of the skies. It was believed that some wairua could follow him.

Another name for this house is Hawaiki-nui [Great Hawaiki].

Hei
An Arawa ancestor

This man was an uncle of Tama-te-kapua, captain of *Te Arawa* on its voyage from Hawaiki. When the ship had arrived and was coasting south, its leading men claimed land for their descendants by identifying a landmark on the shore with some part of their body. While they were passing Whitianga on the eastern shore of Te Paeroa-o-Toi (the Coromandel Peninsula), Hei named a prominent rock after the curve of his nose, in this way laying claim to the coastline in that district. Later he went there to live.

Hei's descendants intermarried with the ancient peoples in the region and became known as Ngāti Hei. His son Waitaha, however, settled in the Tauranga area, and his descendants remained there.

Hikurangi
A sacred mountain

It was believed in some regions that when the hero Māui was pulling up the fish that became the North Island, the first part that rose through the water was a mountain named Hikurangi. This therefore became the first part of the land that the light fell upon.

In another myth, the story of Paikea and Ruatapu who were living in Hawaiki, Paikea is about to travel to Aotearoa when he is warned by his demonic brother Ruatapu that at a certain time he will arrive at Paikea's new home in the form of high waves on the beach, and that people must then run to Mount Hikurangi to escape the flood. This happens, and the crowds upon Hikurangi survive the disaster.

In both these traditions, then, Hikurangi rises above the ocean (a non-human realm associated with danger and destruction). In both stories it is a sacred mountain of great power, in the first because of its primacy and the light that falls upon it, in the second because it is a place of refuge and survival.

As well as existing in mythology, the name Hikurangi was given in reality to a number of prominent hills and mountains in different parts of the country. The best known is Hikurangi on the East Coast, the tapu mountain of Ngāti Porou. At dawn the sun lights up this peak while all around is in darkness, an event that repeats the first occasion on which the sun shone upon Hikurangi as it rose above the waters.

Hina
Māui's sister, or wife

Hina, or Hina-uri, is sometimes the sister of the trickster hero Māui and sometimes his wife instead. As his sister she marries a man named Irawaru, and a quarrel between the two brothers-in-law ends with Māui turning Irawaru into the first dog. Occasionally Hina is so upset at this that she throws herself into the sea, swims for many days, then reaches Tinirau on his island and marries him (although this episode with Tinirau is more often associated with Hine-te-iwaiwa).

When Hina is Māui's wife rather than sister, she has an encounter while bathing with Tuna [Eel], who seduces her. Learning of this, Māui entices Tuna to visit Hina and kills him.

Hine-ahu-one
The woman shaped from sand

In some regions, such as the East Coast and the Urewera, it is said that Tāne, son of Rangi the sky and Papa the earth, modelled a woman for himself from sand (or soil). According to some, the place he chose for this purpose was the mons veneris of his mother, Papa, which is known as 'the sands at Kurawaka' [te one i Kurawaka].

Tāne formed arms, legs, a body, head, and sexual parts, reciting a ritual chant. He breathed life into his woman, and called her Hine-ahu-one [Woman shaped from sand] – or some say Hine-hau-one. Then he took to wife the woman he had made. She bore a daughter, whom he married as well.

Hine-hopu
Ancestor of Ngāti Pikiao

Between Lakes Rotoiti and Rotoehu there was a well-known track, Hine-hopu's Path [Te Ara o Hine-hopu], where waka were portaged. When a Ngā Puhi force under the command of Hongi Hika invaded the region in 1823, they took their own waka up a river near Maketū, through Lake Rotoehu, and over this portage. They then sailed straight through to Lake Rotorua and attacked Mokoia Island, where the people of Te Arawa had sought refuge. Te Arawa put up a strong resistance but it was an unequal fight, since all of Ngā Puhi were armed with muskets while Te Arawa had only a single gun.

Because of these events, Hine-hopu's Path is often known as Hongi's Track. A road has replaced the path. Beside this road there is a tapu tree, a matāī, which is known now as Hine-hopu's wishing tree. Visitors pay this tipua tree the tribute of a green twig, then by making a wish they ask for its assistance.

Hine-hopu is an important ancestor whose husband was Pikiao. Their descendants became the people of Ngāti Pikiao, who belong to the Lake Rotoiti district.

Hine-i-tapeka
Underground fire

Fire in general comes from Mahuika, and is her possession. But volcanic fire, the fire that burns under the earth, was sometimes thought to belong to Mahuika's sister, Hine-i-tapeka. Charred tree trunks embedded in vast pumice deposits on the Kaingaroa Plains were attributed to her activities.

Hine-kōrako
The pale rainbow

Hine-kōrako [Pale woman] sometimes took the form of a pale rainbow, such as the luminous halo often seen around the moon, and sometimes was identified with the moon itself. Along with Hine-te-iwaiwa she assisted women in childbirth.

During the voyage from Hawaiki of the *Tākitimu*, Hine-kōrako stood before the vessel each night as a lunar rainbow, while Kahukura guided it each day in the shape of the rainbow visible by day. Because these two atua had guided and protected *Tākitimu* they were appealed to in later times by deep-sea voyagers.

Hine-kōrako
A female taniwha

The original inhabitants of Te Rēinga on the Wairoa River, and rugged Mount Whakapunake nearby, were a race of taniwha. After some generations a female taniwha, Hine-kōrako, fell in love with a human man, Tāne-kino. They married and had a son, whom they named Taurenga, but Hine-kōrako abandoned her husband and child when some of his relatives made insulting remarks about her ancestry. She went to live under the spectacular Te Rēinga waterfall, and she is still there today.

Hinemoa and Tūtānekai
Famous lovers

Tūtānekai lived long ago on Mokoia Island in Lake Rotorua. His mother was Rangiuru, wife of the leading rangatira Whakaue, but his father was Tūwharetoa, a rangatira who had visited the island during Whakaue's absence. Whakaue forgave his wife and reared the boy as his own son. Nevertheless, Tūtānekai had to contend with the animosity of his three elder half-brothers.

Every year the people living around Lakes Rotorua and Rotoiti gathered at Ōwhata, on the eastern shore. At these meetings the young men would gaze from a distance at the beautiful Hinemoa, high-ranking daughter of two great rangatira, Te Umu-karia and his wife Hine-maru. This woman was tapu, set apart; many men had sought to marry her, among them Whakaue's elder sons, but her people had not yet chosen her husband.

Tūtānekai was also in love with Hinemoa, though he did not imagine she would return his love. But he was a handsome man, and a fine dancer and athlete, and Hinemoa soon fell in love with him.

When Whakaue and his sons returned to Mokoia, Tūtānekai told his father that he wanted Hinemoa and that his love was returned. He built a platform on some rising ground, and every evening he and his friend Tiki sat there and played their flutes.

In the still air their music floated across to Ōwhata, four kilometres away, and Hinemoa knew it came from Tūtānekai. But her people were suspicious, and every evening they dragged up their waka to prevent her from paddling across to Mokoia. One night she made up her mind to swim, despite the distance. She found six empty gourds in a cookhouse and she took off her clothes and entered the water, three gourds under each arm. It was getting dark, but the sound of the flutes told her the way to go.

At last she reached Mokoia and found Wai-kimihia, a thermal pool near the shore. She was shivering with cold, so she warmed herself in the water. As well she was shivering with shame, wondering what Tūtānekai would think and ashamed to be without clothes.

Just then Tūtānekai sent his slave for water. When he passed the pool where Hinemoa sat, she asked in a gruff voice, 'Who is the water for?'

The slave told her, 'Tūtānekai.'

Hinemoa asked for the gourd, drank from it, then broke it. He asked the reason, was given no answer, so went and informed his master. He was sent back again, and once more Hinemoa took the gourd, drank, and broke it.

Furious at this infringement of his tapu, Tūtānekai put on fine cloaks and went to fight the stranger. Hinemoa hid beneath a ledge of rock; Tūtānekai felt around the edge, pulled her out, and discovered she was Hinemoa. He placed a cloak around her, and they went to his house and slept together. This, in those days, signified marriage.

At daybreak everyone was up and working, but Tūtānekai did not appear. A messenger slid aside the window shutter and saw four legs, not two; he ran and told what he had seen, he was sent again, and this time he recognised Hinemoa.

When he shouted his news, the elder brothers would not believe it. Then Tūtānekai came out of his house with Hinemoa beside him. At the same time, across the lake, large waka were seen approaching from Ōwhata. They knew it was Te Umu-karia and they expected war, but the two peoples made peace amid much rejoicing.

Hine-mokemoke
A lonely singer

Long ago, men fishing off Matakaoa Point, near Wharekāhika (Hicks Bay), used to hear strange songs coming up from under the water. One day some fishermen pulled up their anchor and found a pūpūtara [trumpet shell] clinging to it. This shell had been singing the songs they had heard.

The shell was fitted with a mouthpiece and named Hine-mokemoke

[Lonely woman]. It was regarded as a tipua, a being with uncanny powers, and was used as a trumpet for many years.

Hine-nui-te-pō
The woman who brought death

Although they told different stories about her, nearly everyone knew Hine-nui-te-pō [Great woman the night] as the woman who brought death into the world. Some believed that after Tāne had married his daughter, Hine-tītama, she was greatly shamed to discover her father's identity and she ran to the underworld. There, it was often said, her name changed to Hine-nui-te-pō. Tāne followed and begged her to return, but she told him to go back to the world and rear up their offspring. She would remain below to receive them when they died.

It was also believed that the trickster hero Māui determined to overcome death by conquering Hine-nui-te-pō. He approached as she lay sleeping, intending to enter her body by the path through which children enter this world. But the little birds accompanying him laughed when they saw Māui disappearing into the great woman's vagina, and their laughter woke her. She brought her legs together, Māui was crushed to death, and that is why people die now.

Yet Hine-nui-te-pō is also a mother who cares for her children after their death.

Hine-poupou
The woman who swam Raukawa

Hine-poupou and her husband, Te Oripāroa, lived on Kapiti Island, north of Raukawa (Cook Strait). Then after a quarrel, Te Oripāroa crossed the strait with his people and settled on the southern shore, on Rangitoto (D'Urville Island); Hine-poupou's father accompanied him.

Hine-poupou was greatly distressed to find her people gone, and she set out to swim across Raukawa. For many nights and days she swam, resting occasionally on rocks, then quite close to Rangitoto she discovered a rock with taniwha on one side and enormous hāpuku on the other. She swam on, and at last reached the village where her husband and father were living. She warmed herself in the sun, then approached her father's house. Her father wept over her, and at dawn he performed a ceremony recognising their reunion.

She lived with Te Oripāroa once more, but soon he again treated her badly and she decided to take revenge. She told her people about the fishing rock she had found, and they all put to sea to visit it.

When Hine-poupou and her brothers reached the place, they anchored their vessels by the side where the hāpuku lived; when Te Oripāroa and his people arrived, she told him to go to the other side. At the same time she made an offering to the taniwha, and they sent a great wind. Te Oripāroa's people were destroyed, but Hine-poupou's waka returned safely to land.

Sometimes the story ends here, but one storyteller says that Te Oripāroa and his younger brother did not die. Their vessel was blown across the ocean to Hawaiki, and there the brothers encountered an old woman who told them about an immense bird, Te Pouākai, that was preying upon the island's inhabitants.

The two men built a strong house with walls made from trees still rooted in the ground. The younger brother set out to lure Te Pouākai towards the house, it pursued him, and he got there just in time. The enraged bird tried to break down the house, but when it thrust a wing inside, the men cut it off. The other wing went in, and again their weapons came down. Finally Te Pouākai pushed in its head. The brothers swung their weapons and the creature fell dead.

Hine-pūkohurangi
Woman of the mist

In the Urewera Mountains, Hine-pūkohurangi [Sky mist woman] is the mist and her younger sister, Hine-wai [Water woman], the light rain that falls in foggy weather. These women are fairies [tūrehu]. One night they came down from the sky so that Hine-pūkohurangi could visit a human man, Uenuku. At dawn Hine-wai called a warning, and when Uenuku awoke his woman was gone.

After this she visited Uenuku every night. She told him, 'You mustn't say anything about me until we have a child. If you deceive me, I won't stay with you.'

But Uenuku did tell, and his people advised him to stop up the chinks around the door and window so the house would stay dark. That night

Hine-pūkohurangi paid no attention when she heard Hine-wai's warning, because the house was still dark. When the sun was high the people slid the door across, and the woman saw she had been deceived. She sang a song of farewell, then flew up to the sky.

Uenuku searched for her until he died. Then at last he did find her, because he became the rainbow, which accompanies the mist.

According to another tradition, Hine-pūkohurangi married Te Maunga [The mountain]. Their son, Pōtiki, is one of the main ancestors from whom the people of Tūhoe trace descent, and for this reason they are known as the Children of the Mist.

Hine-rauāmoa
Youngest of the Children of Light

In the Urewera Mountains and southern Bay of Plenty, Rangi the sky and Papa the earth were believed to have had three children: Tāne, Tangotango, and Wainui, who is female. Tangotango married Wainui and their six children, known as the Children of Light [Te Whānau Mārama], became the origin of light in its different forms. The youngest, Hine-rauā-moa, who gave only a faint glimmering light, later married her uncle, Tāne, and had eight children. They are Rongo-mā-Tāne, Hine-te-iwaiwa, Tangaroa, Tū, Tāwhirimātea, Haumia, Ioio-whenua and Pū-tē-hue.

Hine-rauāmoa is believed in this region to have initiated the art of weaving.

Hine-rau-whārangi
Plant and human fertility

Hine-rau-whārangi [Woman of widespread leaves] is often a daughter of Tāne and Hine-tītama. She represents and ensures the growth and development of plants, and as well she is one of the early female ancestors who assist women with their tasks and responsibilities—for this became her concern when her mother went to live in the underworld.

Hine-rehia
The discovery of weaving

The Hauraki peoples believed that the techniques of weaving and plaiting were acquired from a fairy [patupaiarehe] woman, Hine-rehia, who married a human man named Karanga-roa. This man was a rangatira of the Maruiwi people who lived on Motuihe Island in Tikapa (the Hauraki Gulf).

Hine-rehia was expert in preparing flax fibre and dyeing it, weaving garments and plaiting baskets and mats, but she worked only at night and on foggy days. At dawn she put away her unfinished work, as the sun would otherwise undo her work and make her lose her skills.

The other women, anxious to acquire Hine-rehia's knowledge, asked a tohunga to make her keep on working after the sun rose. He did so, and Hine-rehia worked on unwittingly while the women, concealed nearby, learnt her secrets. At last she realised that she had been deceived. She sang a farewell to her husband and children, then a cloud came down and bore her off to her home on the Moehau Range.

Hine-ruru
An owl guardian

Families and larger kinship groups recognised the existence of ancestral guardians embodied in animals. These spirits took a variety of forms, but the guardians [kaitiaki] that warn of death are usually owls (moreporks). These have different names.

In Northland they are often known as Hine-ruru [Owl woman]. This special bird has the power to protect, warn and advise. As well as appearing at night when someone is about to die, she may announce the imminent arrival of visitors. If she is seen flying ahead or walking along the road, she is usually there as a protector at a time of danger.

Hine-te-iwaiwa
The model wife and mother

The powers and responsibilities of women were established in the beginning by Hine-te-iwaiwa. This early ancestor is the woman who provided the pattern that women now follow. All girls were dedicated to her at birth.

A myth tells of Hine-te-iwaiwa's journey to find Tinirau, the handsome rangatira she has decided to marry. She swims through the ocean for many days to reach his home on Motu-tapu [Sacred island], becomes his wife, and presently has his child.

Women in childbirth were aided by the recitation of a ritual chant believed to have been repeated for the first time when Hine-te-iwaiwa was giving birth to her son Tūhuruhuru. This chant associates the woman with Hine-te-iwaiwa, who provided the precedent and has the power now to help her.

Hine-te-iwaiwa was one of the ancestors who gave a girl strength when her lips were being tattooed. She was often thought to have introduced the art of weaving (though other women, more specialised figures, were also associated with this).

She was sometimes believed to have been the first woman to act as a ruahine, a role performed by a high-ranking woman when taking part in a ritual to remove an excess of tapu. In removing much of the tapu of a new house so that people could safely live in it, Hine-te-iwaiwa established a precedent that has been followed ever since.

Hine-tītama
Tāne's daughter

After Tāne formed the first woman from the soil of Hawaiki, he married her and they had a beautiful daughter. In many versions of the story, this girl was Hine-tītama.

When his daughter grew up, Tāne took her to wife as well. She bore him children, but then was greatly shamed to discover he was her father as well as her husband. She ran down to the underworld, and there her name changed, it is often said, to Hine-nui-te-pō [Great woman the night]. Tāne followed and begged her to return, but she told him that he must go back to the world and rear up their offspring, and that she would remain below to receive them when they died.

Hine-tua-hōanga
The sandstone woman

Sandstone was an important resource for shaping, polishing and sharpening stone tools and ornaments. Usually it was regarded as a woman, Hine-tua-hōanga [Sandstone woman].

The use of sandstone was established in the beginning by the hero Rata, when he had to avenge his father. To do this he needed a waka, and to build his waka he needed a sharp adze. His mother, Hine-tua-hōanga, advised him how to achieve this; Rata did as she told him, then sailed to take his revenge.

Sandstone deposits are present in Aotearoa because Hine-tua-hōanga left Hawaiki to pursue over the ocean a fish, Ngahue's pet, which later became greenstone. After a struggle between Hine-tua-hōanga and Ngahue, she took up her residence in this land.

Hine-waiapu
A supernatural boulder

The Waiapu River and its valley, near East Cape, are said to take their name from a boulder named Hine-waiapu [Waiapu woman] that lies at the river mouth. This boulder is a tipua, an entity with extraordinary powers. She consists of siliceous stone known as waiapu, and was placed there by Hine-tua-hōhanga [Sandstone woman] during her struggle long ago with Ngahue. At the same time, Hine-tua-hōhanga introduced other supplies of waiapu to the region.

This stone was a valued resource, employed in polishing stone adzes.

Hingānga-roa
Founder of a house of learning

A great woodcarver, Hingānga-roa founded at Ūawa (Tolaga Bay) a famous house of learning [whare wānanga] known as Te Rāwheoro, where both carving and history were taught. He married Iranui, sister of Kahungunu, and they had three sons. The youngest, Hauiti, fought with his brothers Taua and Māhaki, who eventually left the district and settled elsewhere. Hauiti remained at Ūawa and became the founding ancestor of Te Aitanga-a-Hauiti.

Horoirangi
An Arawa ancestor

An early ancestor of the Uenuku-kōpako people in the Rotorua district, Horoirangi lived about four hundred years ago. At Te Whetengu, a pā on a hill named Te Tihi-o-Tonga, her stone image, carved in a hidden recess in a cliff, became the mauri (source of fertility) of the lands owned by the people there. She also ensured the vitality of her descendants.

Horoirangi was not, however, responsible for the conduct of warfare. This was under the control of a male deity, Maru-te-whare-aitu, whose emblem lay in a tapu enclosure nearby.

Horo-matangi
A taniwha in Lake Taupō

This fierce taniwha lives in an underwater cave by Motutaiko, an island in Lake Taupō. In earlier times he was believed to assume the form of a reptile, or sometimes to take the form of a black rock. Some said he was an old man red as fire.

Two stone dogs high up on the Karangahape cliffs, on the lake's western shore, were associated with the taniwha. These dogs were never seen but might be heard howling on misty mornings.

Horouta
An East Coast waka

Some tohunga of Ngāti Porou said that the *Horouta* set out for Aotearoa from Hawaiki. Others taught that this waka sailed first from the east coast of Aotearoa, acquired the kūmara in Hawaiki, then made a return voyage.

In one version of the story, the early ancestor Toi, who did not possess the kūmara, lived at Whitianga (Mercury Bay). There he was visited by Kahukura and Rongo-i-amo, who had arrived by magical means from Hawaiki. These men gave Toi some dried kūmara and he liked it so much that he arranged for his waka, the *Horouta*, to make a voyage to Hawaiki to acquire the kūmara. Kahukura led this expedition.

At Hawaiki the crew took their vessel alongside cliffs consisting entirely of kūmara. Kahukura recited a ritual chant and thrust in his digging stick, and the cliffs of Hawaiki slid down until the waka was full of kūmara.

The return voyage was led by a man named Pawa (or Paoa). Before the crew set sail, Kahukura warned them never to allow the kūmara to come into contact with fernroot (for these two plants must always be kept apart). But when the *Horouta* made landfall at Ahuahu (Great Mercury Island), a woman named Kanawa disregarded these instructions. She stole some fernroot and hid it on board when the ship sailed on.

The *Horouta* was now coasting south, distributing kūmara, but the gods were angry at Kanawa's breach of tapu and they sent a storm. Just outside Whakatāne, near the Ōhiwa Harbour, the woman was flung into the water by the waves. She rose and seized the bow of the waka, the vessel overturned, and she died there.

The ship was cast up on the shore, its bowpiece damaged. Some were assigned to guard it while Pawa led a party into the interior. There he felled a tree and adzed a new bowpiece, and his companions snared and speared birds so they would have good food to offer to the men who would soon be working on the ship.

But when all was ready, Pawa and his men learnt that the vessel had been repaired without them and had sailed on around the East Coast. Then they set off along the shore, hoping to catch up. They did not succeed in this, but Pawa created many landmarks that are still to be seen. Meanwhile the *Horouta* continued to distribute kūmara to places that it passed.

Hotumauea
A very tall man

This ancestor of the Waikato peoples was very tall and could jump prodigious distances. One day he and his wife, with their baby son, were down in a pit in some sand dunes, drawing water from a spring, when his treacherous brothers-in-law came to kill him. The men surrounded the pit and there seemed no way for Hotumauea to escape. But he gave a great leap, reached the top, and was gone.

The brothers-in-law pursued Hotumauea to the bank of the Waikato River, and thought they had him cornered. But he leapt to the top of a tawa tree, then jumped right across the great river. On the far side his feet sank into the rock and his footprints are still there now.

Hotupuku
A taniwha at Kaingaroa

On the Kaingaroa Plains, a taniwha named Hotupuku used to prey upon travellers passing through the region. At last their relatives at Taupō went to investigate. When they reached the place where Hotupuku lived, the taniwha smelt human flesh and emerged from his den. They fled, and some survived and some did not.

When the news reached Rotorua, a party of men from Ngāti Tama set out to fight Hotupuku. They plaited a rope and made a large noose, then some went forward to entice the taniwha from his den. Hotupuku thundered towards them, the decoys ran through the noose, and the rope was pulled tight. Hotupuku lashed about but could do nothing. Soon he lay dead.

The warriors saw that the taniwha looked like a tuatara, though in size he was like a whale. They ate their enemy, then returned to their homes at Ōhinemutu .

Houmea
An evil woman

This wicked woman was really an atua, a spirit, but at first her family did not realise this. When her husband, Uta, returned from fishing, she would swallow down all the fish he had caught, then pretend they had been stolen by a war party. In the end her two sons, Tū-tawake and Nini, discovered what she was doing. In revenge she swallowed them down as well, but Uta recited a ritual chant that brought them up again.

Uta tried to escape with his boys, but she entered a shag and pursued their waka. When she reached them, her throat gaping wide, the boys had hidden their father and had roasted a fish on a fire. They gave her this fish to eat, then they threw down her throat a hot stone from the fireplace, and the monster died. She lives now in the form of a shag, and the name Houmea is given to evil, thievish women in this world.

Houses of learning
Famous schools and teachers

Sons of high-ranking men, especially the elder sons, often attended a formal course of instruction in history, genealogy, religious practices and other subjects at a house of learning [whare wānanga, or whare kura]. They were taught by leading tohunga, generally in the winter months. The subjects taught included traditions and ritual chants which were not communicated to other persons.

A building was set aside for the purpose, and a strict tapu governed the actions of teachers and students. Much ritual surrounded the students' entrance to the school and the conditions under which they lived during their period of instruction.

Young men of high rank might also have esoteric knowledge communicated to them privately by their fathers or grandfathers. Often this information was imparted to the eldest son, though in some high-ranking families a younger son might be chosen.

But high-ranking youths were not the only ones to receive formal instruction. All young people were taught skills such as martial arts, horticulture, the manufacture of implements, fishing, bird-hunting and weaving (some of these skills being appropriate for males and others for females). As well, boys and girls received much of their education by watching their relatives at work and assisting them. Even the less privileged had a great many practical skills and a general knowledge of history and tradition.

Humuhumu
A taniwha guardian

This is one of the taniwha that escorted the *Māhuhu* on its voyage from Hawaiki. Later he accompanied his people, Ngāti Whātua, to the Kaipara district and lived in a lagoon at the North Kaipara Heads. His sign was a tōtara log that drifted about there for many generations, moving against the currents and the wind.

Īhenga
An explorer

A grandson of Tama-te-kapua, captain of *Te Arawa*, Īhenga is generally said to have arrived with him from Hawaiki. He lived for a time on the Moehau Range, then returned to Maketū and married Hine-te-kakara, daughter of his uncle Kahu-mata-momoe. He is best known as an explorer.

Hunting kiwi in the interior with his dog Pōtaka-tawhiti, Īhenga discovered Lake Rotoiti and Lake Rotorua. Another Arawa immigrant, Tua-Rotorua, was already living with his people among the hot springs at Ōhinemutu, but Īhenga tricked Tua-Rotorua into believing he had the prior claim.

Mount Ngongotahā, quite close to Ōhinemutu, at this time had fairies [patupaiarehe] living on its heights. Climbing the mountain, Īhenga discovered the fairies' pā on the summit. He was thirsty, and asked for water; a woman offered a drink from her gourd, and because of this he later named the mountain Ngongo-tahā [Drink from gourd]. When the fairies crowded around, Īhenga became frightened and fled down the mountain. Later, though, he became very friendly with them.

Īhenga's last journey was undertaken with his uncle, Kahu-mata-momoe, to visit two of his brothers in the Far North and another brother at Moehau. With some companions, he and his uncle crossed to the west coast, walked north, then later returned through Tāmaki and Moehau.

Io
A high god

New resources, technologies and contacts began changing Māori life and thought early in the nineteenth century, then in the 1830s and '40s most Māori people became Christian. In 1840 the country came under British rule, and hitherto inconceivable numbers of Pākehā settlers began arriving and demanding land. By the late 1850s it was clear that the country was being overrun and that the government's main concern was to protect Pākehā interests.

In this highly stressful situation, Māori society and thought survived through the creative adaptation of new ideas. While many peoples remained with the missionaries and the government, in several parts of the country religious leaders (notably Te Ua and Te Kooti) founded new faiths.

These made much use of traditional concepts but were mainly Christian, in that they were based upon interpretations of the Bible. Initially at least, some of these faiths were associated with armed resistance. They were shaped by a need for religious and intellectual independence from Pākehā, and a strong desire for political power.

Another approach was to modify and extend traditional beliefs so that they became a viable alternative to Christianity. This was the direction taken, from the late 1850s onward, by a group of Ngāti Kahungunu thinkers in the Wairarapa and Hawke's Bay whose leader was initially the tohunga Te Mātorohanga. Long afterwards, in 1913 and 1915, materials derived from their records were published in a two-volume work, *The Lore of the Whare Wānanga*. Percy Smith, a Pākehā scholar, contributed an inexact translation and a commentary.

Much in these writings is new, yet most of these myths have their origin in the earlier traditions of a cultural region that extended around the coastal areas of the southernmost part of the North Island. The main difference is the presence of the high god Io, a figure not mentioned in earlier writings.

Despite his great power and status, Io is not presented as all-powerful; it seems inappropriate for Percy Smith to describe him as supreme. He is not, for instance, responsible for the creation of Rangi the sky and Papa the earth. In the beginning these two simply exist.

Rangi-nui and Papa have seventy sons. Above Rangi-nui there are eleven other skies; Io lives in the highest sky, known as Tikitiki-o-ngā-rangi. When Tāne begins an ascent to Io, his jealous elder brother Whiro attempts to precede him. But the winds (Tāwhirimātea and his offspring) blow Tāne upward until he stands at last in the presence of Io. He asks for the three baskets [kete] of knowledge, and Io gives them to him; they contain all wisdom [wānanga], with directions as to how the world should be ordered.

Back on earth, Tāne places his baskets within the first house of learning, which he has already built in readiness for this. He then undertakes the governance of the earth.

There follows a war with the evil Whiro and his faction. Tāne and his companions win this war, and Whiro goes down to the underworld, from where he wages continual war against all beings on the earth. Tāne, however, with assistance from Io and from his brothers, now creates the first woman, Hine-ahu-one. He takes her to wife and their descendants are human beings.

These beliefs spread from the Wairarapa, changing somewhat as they did so. By the time *The Lore of the Whare Wananga* appeared, belief in Io had lessened considerably in the Wairarapa. But the publication of this work led to further Māori interest in Io, and belief in him, in many parts of the country.

In the Waikato region, within the King Movement, beliefs concerning Io had meanwhile taken a rather different course, one much influenced by earlier Tainui tradition. *King Potatau*, a book published in 1960 by Pei Te Hurinui, presents esoteric teachings taken from manuscripts dating, it seems, from the late nineteenth century. Here Io becomes fully evolved only after two entities, Hani and Puna, are merged within him. Hani and Puna embody and represent respectively the male essence and the female essence, so that Io now possesses both male and female powers. Later, Tāwhaki (rather than Tāne) ascends to the highest sky and returns with the baskets of knowledge.

Ioio-whenua
A peacemaker

Among Tūhoe in the Urewera mountains and Ngāti Awa in the southern Bay of Plenty, Ioio-whenua is a son of Tāne and Hine-rauāmoa. When others began to stir up strife he made peace, being associated in this undertaking with Rongo and, some say, Haumia and Pū-tē-hue. These last three are personifications of food plants – which is appropriate, since horticulture was traditionally a peaceful pursuit. It is not known whether Ioio-whenua was also involved especially with the cultivation of food.

Irakau
A woman of great mana

Irakau had mana over all the creatures in the ocean, including whales and taniwha. This was not surprising, since her father was the famous Raka-taura who had ridden from Hawaiki on the back of a taniwha. Her mother belonged to the earliest peoples in the land.

Irakau was the main ancestor of the Waitaha people on the shores of the Hauraki Gulf, and she passed on her powers to them. These people possessed therefore a special relationship with whales. On the coast, at a highly tapu place named Rangiriri, a mauri for whales represented and contained the life force of these great creatures. It took the visible form of a sandbank, overgrown with coastal grasses, which resembled a whale with its head pointing inland. Whales from all over the ocean were drawn to this supernatural whale.

Irākewa
A precursor

As Irākewa lay sleeping one night in Hawaiki, his wairua went out across the water to Aotearoa; it visited Whakatāne and other places, then returned. Irākewa awoke and told his people, 'There is a land far away that is a good land for you to go to. There is a waterfall in that place, and a cave on the hillside, and the rock standing in the river there is myself.'

So his people sailed from Hawaiki on the *Mātaatua*. At Whakatāne they found the waterfall, and the cave, which became a home for the captain's sister Muriwai, and at the entrance to the river they saw the rock that is Irākewa. They settled there and became ancestors of Ngāti Awa.

Irawaru
The first dog

Irawaru began life as a man, but then his sister married the trickster Māui, the two men quarrelled, and Māui turned Irawaru into a dog. According to one story, this happened because Māui coveted Irawaru's dogtail cape. He offered to tattoo Irawaru's lips, then with Irawaru at his mercy he pulled out his back, tail, nose and ears, forequarters and hindquarters. He recited a ritual chant, and Irawaru became the first dog. Because of the tattooing, dogs have dark noses and lips.

Iwi-katere
Owner of a wise bird

Tūī were often kept in cages and taught words and songs. Long ago at Te Wairoa (Wairoa), a rangatira named Iwi-katere owned a pet tūī he taught ritual chants of every kind. The bird became so knowledgeable that it recited all the chants at the rituals performed at harvest time.

One year a neighbouring rangatira, Tama-te-rā, sent a messenger to ask if the bird could officiate at his kūmara-harvest ceremony. Iwi-katere agreed, but said that the bird would first have to perform his own ceremony. Regarding this as an insult, Tama-te-rā that night sent a man to steal the bird.

When Iwi-katere discovered his loss, he knew Tama-te-rā was to blame and he raised an army. In the end the thief's people left Te Wairoa and migrated to Heretaunga (Hawke's Bay).

Kahukura
The discovery of net-making

In the Far North the knowledge of net-making was acquired from the fairies [patupaiarehe] by Kahukura. On the beach at Rangiaohia, in Tokerau (Doubtless Bay), this man saw where the fairies had been fishing, so he returned that night and found them netting mackerel. He worked alongside them, unobserved, until at dawn the fish were brought up on the beach and the fairies started tying them together, threading strings through the gills.

Kahukura was tying his fish as well, but he used a slip-knot, so when his string was loaded with fish they all fell off. He started again, and a fairy came up and tied the knot for him, but afterwards Kahukura untied the knot and let the fish slip off again. He kept delaying them like this until the dawn. Then the fairies discovered Kahukura and fled, leaving behind their fish, net and waka.

Kahukura took the net and used it as a pattern. He learnt to tie knots and he taught net-making to his sons.

Kahukura
A powerful god

At Waiapu on the East Coast, the tohunga Pita Kāpiti taught that Kahukura was an atua, in the form of a man, who travelled by magical means from Hawaiki to Aotearoa. With a companion, Rongo-i-amo, he visited the early ancestor Toi at Whitianga and introduced him to the kūmara. To acquire seed kūmara for Toi, he then led a voyage to Hawaiki on the *Horouta*.

There he gave the crew the kūmara, and they afterwards returned without him.

Other peoples have other stories. Often Kahukura is a war god, and the rainbow comes as his sign. He was the main god brought on the *Tākitimu* from Hawaiki. Elsewhere, as among the Tainui peoples, he was identified with the great Uenuku, whose sign is also the rainbow.

Kahukura
A sorcerer

In many places Kahukura was a war god, while at Waiapu he was regarded as a god who brought the kūmara (see the previous entry). At Ūawa (Tolaga Bay), the tohunga Mohi Ruatapu recognised the existence of more than one Kahukura, but writes only about an early ancestor of this name who is a son of Tangaroa. The rest of Tangaroa's children are fish, but Kahukura takes the form of a man, and some humans are descended from him. He is known mainly as the origin of a ritual chant that strikes people down.

Kahu-mata-momoe
An early Arawa ancestor

This man came from Hawaiki on *Te Arawa*, being a son of its captain Tama-te-kapua; he settled at Maketū (in the Bay of Plenty), where *Te Arawa* made landfall. Afterwards a dispute arose between Kahu and Tama-te-kapua as to the ownership of a kūmara plantation, and this led to Tama-te-kapua's going to live on the Moehau Range. Then there was another struggle and Kahu's elder brother, Tūhoro-mata-kakā, abandoned Maketū and joined Tama-te-kapua.

Much later, Tūhoro-mata-kakā's son Īhenga had need of Kahu-mata-momoe. When Tūhoro-mata-kakā lay dying, he told Īhenga that after carrying out the rituals associated with his death he must journey to Maketū, where his uncle would remove the consequent tapu. So at the proper time Īhenga journeyed to Maketū and boldly entered Kahu's house. Kahu was told of the intruder and ran to kill him, but he saw the resemblance to his brother and he wept over his nephew. Afterwards Īhenga married Kahu-mata-momoe's daughter Hine-te-kakara.

Some time later Īhenga settled by Lake Rotorua, and Kahu joined him there. Then Kahu decided to travel to the Far North to visit his nephews, Taramainuku and Warenga. Kahu and Īhenga made the journey together, then Kahu returned to Rotorua through Tāmaki and Moehau. Finally as an old man he returned to Maketū and died there.

Kahungunu
Founder of a numerous people

Kahungunu was a man like no other. A son of the famous Tamatea, he made his way in the world not as a warrior, but through his ability as a provider and through a series of marriages to attractive and important women.

He is often said to have been born in Kaitaia. While he was still young his father removed his household to Tauranga, and there he grew to manhood in the company of his elder half-brother, Whāene. Finally he quarrelled with Whāene and went to Ōpōtiki, where he lived with relatives. Then he set out again, making his way around the east coast. Eventually he reached Tūranga-nui (the Gisborne district) and married a daughter of the great rangatira Ruapani; it is usually said that she was Ruapani's eldest child Ruarauhanga, and that she bore Kahungunu two sons. But presently he became restless and moved further south. At Whareongaonga he married two sisters and had two more children.

All this time he had been hearing about Rongomai-wahine, a beautiful high-ranking woman at Tawapata on the Māhia Peninsula, and eventually he visited her people. On his arrival he found that she had just married a man named Tama-taku-tai. But he was not dismayed, and he started thinking how he could win her.

He decided he would do it with food. He took his men to dig fernroot on the mountains, and they came back with large bundles. They let these fall over a cliff and right down into the village; all the people were impressed, and came eagerly to get their share. Then Kahungunu had another idea. The people had to get their pāua from deep water where diving was difficult; he dived down and filled a large basket, and repeated this feat until there were shellfish enough for the whole village. Once more the women were loud in their praise.

Then Kahungunu told his men, 'When you eat the pāua, keep the roes for me.'

He ate the roes till his stomach was full, then went as usual to the house shared by Tama-taku-tai and Rongomai-wahine; his bed was on one side and theirs on the other. Then the wind in Kahungunu's stomach rose up because of the pāua. The scoundrel got up and boldly went over to the two of them as they lay sleeping; he pulled up the cloaks that covered them, let go a fart, then put them back again. When the stench hit their noses, the man and his wife jumped up and started quarrelling, each blaming the other.

After a while they lay down again, while Kahungunu laughed to himself. Presently he went over and did the same thing again. This time there was a serious quarrel and the man spoke ill of his wife's parents and brothers. So the woman went off to tell her parents, who were deeply upset.

Some writers say that Rongomai-wahine was given to Kahungunu at this point, others that this happened after Kahungunu managed to drown Tama-taku-tai next day while he was surfing in a small waka. Certainly Kahungunu married her, and stayed with her. She bore him two sons and two daughters.

There are conflicting stories about Kahungunu; some writers name other wives and children besides those mentioned here. Many of his children became important ancestors. Through his son Kahukuranui, Kahungunu was the founder of Ngāti Kahungunu, whose numerous divisions extend from Wairoa southwards through Heretaunga (Hawke's Bay) to the Wairarapa.

Kaiwhare
A taniwha near Piha

This taniwha lives in an underwater cave just south of Piha. He used to visit the Manukau Harbour to receive offerings from the people there, and at first he treated them well. But then, for some reason, he began killing and eating men and women who were fishing and gathering shell-fish, and it became too dangerous to go out on the harbour. The people were desperate. At last they heard of Tāmure, a man at Hauraki who possessed a mere with special powers.

Tāmure agreed to help them. He sent some men out spearing flounder, and hid near Kaiwhare's den. Seeing the men's torches, the taniwha began to stir, and as he emerged Tāmure struck him with his weapon. The wounded creature was allowed to live, and afterwards contented himself with crayfish and octopuses caught near his cave.

Kametara
A man with a demon wife

Kametara married a woman who bore him a boy and a girl. Then another woman, a tipua [demon], made her appearance. Not knowing what she was, Kametara married her as well.

The demon woman attempted to murder her human co-wife. When they were fishing out at sea she told her to dive to free their anchor, then she cut the rope and paddled off.

But the woman did not drown. She swam to an uninhabited island and survived by eating shellfish and plant foods. She built herself a house, and wove garments. She was pregnant at the time and she presently gave birth to twin boys, whom she reared carefully.

She composed a song lamenting her separation from her people and her husband, and she taught it to her sons. When they were old enough, she told them to fell a tree and adze a waka; they did this, and set out to find their relatives. Presently they met them, and revealed their identity by singing their mother's lament. They did not see their father, who was living at the home of his demon wife.

The brothers returned to their mother and soon their relatives followed. During the woman's years on the island she had worked so industriously that she was able now to appear clothed in beautiful garments, and to offer her relatives gifts of garments and fine food. Then they all lived permanently on the island.

Kapu-manawa-whiti
Hidden intentions

Kapu belonged to Ngāti Raukawa and Ngāti Maniapoto. His full name, Kapu-manawa-whiti [Kapu-with-hidden-intentions], indicates his well-earned reputation as a schemer.

The Waikato people tell about a time when Tūhourangi, from Lake Rotorua, came with a retinue to visit Kapu, arriving unexpectedly in the early summer when food was scarce. This was embarrassing, and Kapu wanted revenge. When Tūhourangi invited him to return the visit, he set out almost immediately with a large party. He reached Rotorua soon after Tūhourangi, and the people were ashamed because they had little to give them.

During this visit the two rangatira talked about food. Tūhourangi said he liked preserved birds best, but Kapu maintained that water was best of all. Afterwards he surprised Tūhourangi by inviting him to visit him again, suggesting the early summer.

Kapu prepared for Tūhourangi's arrival by laying in stores of preserved game and by building a pā on a site far from water. When all was ready his people built a house and dug a well inside it.

Tūhourangi duly arrived and was feasted upon his favourite foods. Soon he became thirsty, but all the streams had dried up in the summer weather. Tūhourangi was crying and groaning – yet there was water in that very house. Kapu had been sitting on the cover. Now he reminded Tūhourangi that he had said water was best, then leapt to one side and offered him a drink.

Tūhourangi realised then that the best food really is water. He went back home very unhappy at being twice overcome by Kapu.

Karitehe
An uncanny people

These yellow-haired, white-skinned people lived in the forests of the Far North, some of them in the Kauhoehoe Caves. Sometimes they would seize human girls who were out gathering the edible bracts of the kiekie flowers – for the Karitehe were often up among these climbing plants, high in the trees. The girls they caught were never seen again.

Kataore
Hinemihi's pet

Most authorities say that Kataore was a taniwha living in a cave overlooking Lake Tikitapu (the Blue Lake) at Te Wairoa. The people there were Tūhourangi, and Kataore was owned by a high-ranking woman, Hinemihi.

These people thought Kataore quite harmless because he always behaved well when they went to feed him – but when travellers approached, he would rush out and devour them. In the end he was destroyed by warriors of Ngāti Tama. Some say their leader, Pitaka, lured Kataore into a snare, others that his chants incapacitated the monster and allowed his companions to spear him to death.

Kaukau-matua
A treasured heirloom

In several myths this greenstone ear pendant is shaped by Ngahue in Hawaiki, brought to Aotearoa by the captain of an ancestral waka, and passed down through the generations. One tradition has Kaukau-matua brought on *Te Arawa* by Tama-te-kapua. In another account it came on the *Tainui*.

Kawharu
The Kaipara giant

This great warrior was four spans tall, about eight metres, and is believed to have lived in the second half of the seventeenth century. He won many battles in the Kaipara region for his Ngāti Whātua people, who had moved south from Hokianga, but he was eventually murdered by his sister's relatives.

His people by this time were living in the northern part of the Kaipara, while the Kawerau people still occupied the southern section. Kawharu's sister had married a Kawerau man, and Kawharu went to visit her. According to custom this should have been quite safe, but the Kawerau treacherously attacked their guests and blocked the gateway. Kawharu climbed the three rows of palisades, but as he was jumping from the last palisade he was caught and killed.

Other authorities, however, maintain that Kawharu was born at Kāwhia and that he won fame there before being visited by a party of Ngāti Whātua and asked for his assistance.

Kēhua
Supernatural visitors

The word kēhua, meaning 'ghost,' seems to have entered the language in about the 1850s. Before this, apparitions had generally been termed wairua. This word remained in use, but now people sometimes spoke of kēhua instead.

There was much debate about the nature of kēhua, and this reflected an uncertainty about the nature of supernatural beings which many people were experiencing at the time. Often they were thought to be souls of the dead (which in the past had always been known as wairua). They were believed to be encountered especially in the Far North while making their way to Te Rēinga.

Kiharoa
A giant in the southern Waikato

This warrior was twice the height of an ordinary man. A rangatira of two related peoples, Ngāti Raukawa and Ngāti Whakatere, he lived in about 1800 at Tokanui Pā, just south of the present town of Te Awamutu. For a long time he was thought invincible. But as he went into battle one day, he slipped and fell on karaka fruit lying on the path. This was a bad omen and despite his great size he was soon overcome.

Kiki and Tāmure
A trial of strength

Kiki, who lived on the Waikato River, was a sorcerer so powerful that his fame spread throughout the country. Another formidable tohunga, Tāmure, decided to challenge his powers. Leaving his Kāwhia home with his daughter and two men, he made his way downriver to Kiki's village, all the time reciting ritual chants.

Kiki called a welcome and they went forward on to the marae. Some of Kiki's people began to cook food for them – but they did so in a tapu oven. Knowing the food was bewitched, Tāmure gave it to his daughter, who as a female had the power to destroy its tapu. Kiki had remained in his house; Tāmure, seated outside, quietly recited chants to destroy him.

Soon Tāmure told his companions to launch their waka, and they paddled off quickly. Meanwhile Kiki became ill. His people knew Tāmure was responsible and they pursued him, but could not catch him. And before long Kiki died, defeated by Tāmure.

Kiwa
An early Tūranga ancestor

Many East Coast authorities consider that Kiwa captained a waka on its voyage from Hawaiki to Tūranga (the Gisborne district); some say it was the *Tākitimu*, others the *Horouta* or the *Hirauta*. The region is sometimes known as Tūranga-nui-a-Kiwa [Great Tūranga of Kiwa] in recognition of Kiwa's role as a founding ancestor.

Kiwa
Guardian of the ocean

In some East Coast traditions the sea is a female, Hine-moana [Ocean woman], and her husband is Kiwa. These two are often said to have had a number of children, who became the origin of different kinds of beings that live in the ocean.

Others, though, say that Kiwa is the brother of Hine-moana, or her guardian, and that he is married to Parawhenuamea (who is the waters that flow from the land to the sea).

A poetic, rhetorical name for the sea is Te Moana Nui a Kiwa [The great ocean of Kiwa].

Kiwi
Powerful ruler of Tāmaki

The Tāmaki Isthmus, where Auckland now stands, was always much coveted for its fertile soil, good climate, and excellent fishing and shellfish beds. By the sixteenth century many of the extinct volcanic cones had become pā, with wide terraces and high scarps cut into their steep slopes. The largest was on the highest hill, Maunga-kiekie (One Tree Hill).

Kiwi was born into the ruling family in the early eighteenth century and lived mainly on Maunga-kiekie; his father was Te Ika-mau-poho and his mother Te Tahuri. As a young man he became ruler of Tāmaki.

Few dangers threatened his people, Te Waiohua; although Ngāti Whātua in the north-west had become powerful, Te Waiohua were so numerous that with good diplomacy they would have continued to occupy their lands in peace. But Kiwi possessed an arrogant and turbulent disposition. At a friendly meeting with Ngāti Whātua he and some companions treacherously killed a number of rangatira, confident that their people's great numbers would save them.

There followed a series of battles in which Te Waiohua were overcome by Ngāti Whātua and driven from the region. In about 1750, Ngāti Whātua took possession of most of the isthmus.

Kōhine-mataroa
A northern ancestor

This woman was the daughter of Puna-te-ariari, sister of the early ancestor Rāhiri. She crossed from South Hokianga to the northern side of the harbour, explored the region, and named all the places she found. She was a skilled gardener, and in suitable areas she established plantations of kūmara and taro.

Kōhine-mataroa married Kaharau, a son of Rāhiri by his second wife Whakaruru. Numerous peoples in the region trace their descent from these ancestors.

Kōkako
A Tainui ancestor

This sixteenth-century rangatira lived south of the Manukau Heads, then later in the interior. Some authorities say that he was responsible for the death of a rival rangatira, Tūheitia.

During a visit to Kāwhia, Kōkako one night forced his attentions upon a woman, Whaea-tapoko, who was drawing water from a spring. Afterwards he told her that if she had a son, he was to be named Tama-inu-pō [Boy drink in the night]; if the child was a daughter, she would be Pare-inu-pō [Girl drink in the night]. He then returned home. The child was a boy and was named accordingly.

When Tama-inu-pō grew to manhood he visited Māhanga, a rangatira at Pūrākau north of Mount Pirongia. He married this man's daughter, Tūkōtuku, and lived there with him.

Māhanga was the son of Tūheitia, whom Kōkako had killed many years previously, and to revenge his father's death he was planning to lead an army against Kōkako. Tama-inu-pō, who had not revealed his father's name, joined this expedition.

After fierce fighting, Māhanga's forces entered Kōkako's pā. Tama-inu-pō found Kōkako, recognising him by his red cloak, and without revealing his identity he overcame him and allowed him to escape. Later he managed to convince Māhanga that he had killed Kōkako, and the army returned.

Some time after these events a son was born to Tama-inu-pō and Tūkōtuku. Since it was necessary for the father's father to take part in the tohi ceremony to be performed over the infant, Māhanga asked Tama-inu-pō about his father. To his great surprise he learnt that Tama-inu-pō's father was Kōkako, and that he was still alive.

Tama-inu-pō determined to visit his father, in the company only of his wife and son, in an attempt to make peace. Māhanga agreed to this and indicated that he would be happy with such an outcome. So Tama-inu-pō, with his wife and child, travelled down the Waikato River. On an island near Rangiriri where Kōkako was now living, Tama-inu-pō confronted his father and revealed his identity. He then led forward his wife – daughter of his father's enemy – and held out their son.

Kokako at once performed the tohi ceremony over his grandson, naming him Wairere, and he agreed to visit Māhanga. At Pūrākau the two rangatira made peace with ritual and festivity.

Kōpū
The morning star

The planet Venus, seen before dawn in the eastern sky, was often known as Kōpū. The brightest of the visible 'stars' [whetū], it was thought to rise as a sign that daylight was coming. Its size and beauty made it the focus of much emotion.

Another name for the morning star is Tāwera. The evening star is usually Meremere.

Kōpūwai
A dog-headed monster

This creature had a man's body but a dog's head, and was covered in scales. He lived with his pack of two-headed dogs in rugged country in the upper reaches of the Matau (Clutha) River, where he hunted human beings.

During the winters the local people lived near the coast, but in the warm months they travelled inland to gather plant foods, snare weka and catch ducks and eels. Many were then the victims of Kōpūwai and his terrible dogs.

On one occasion, having caught a woman named Kaiamio, Kōpūwai decided to keep her as a slave wife. Every day Kaiamio left the monster's cave to draw water from the river and perform other tasks. For many years she lived like that, then she devised a plan. By the river she lashed raupō stalks into bundles and built a raft, then she waited for a north-west wind to bring hot, enervating weather – for she knew Kōpūwai would then lie drowsing in his cave. When the wind came, she launched her raft and the great river carried her to her home. Behind her, Kōpūwai awoke too late and discovered his loss.

Kaiamio's people were astonished and delighted to find her alive. She told her story and they planned their revenge. When the summer was well advanced they made their way up river, then waited for a north-west wind. When it came, Kaiamio approached the cave and found Kōpūwai and the dogs asleep. Some of the men hid by a hole in the roof of the cave while the others piled raupō at the entrance and set it alight. Kōpūwai tried to climb through the roof, but the men battered his fearful head to pieces. Most of his dogs were killed as well.

Some say Kōpūwai is now a pillar of rock on the highest part of The Old Man Range.

Korotangi
A bird lost and found

In a song known to the Tainui peoples and some others, a poet mourns the loss of his pet, a beautiful bird named Korotangi. In his absence his wife had ill-treated Korotangi and the angry bird had escaped. The man searched for his pet but found only a few feathers. He kept these in a carved box, and he composed a lament that was soon widely known.

A stone bird of unknown origin, carved in a style that is not Māori, was discovered in the Waikato district in about 1879, reportedly among the roots of a mānuka tree blown down in a gale. This bird was at once recognised by leading rangatira as being Korotangi, now turned to stone. The people wept over their bird, singing the old lament, and it was explained by some that this treasure had been brought on the *Tainui* from Hawaiki.

Kūī
An ancient woman

In Hokianga it was believed that the first inhabitants in the region, Tuputupu-whenua and his wife Kūī, still lived there under the ground. Kūī now took the form of an insect, named kūī, which lives in holes in the ground (this is the larva of the tiger beetle). A man building a house would make an offering of grass to Kūī, presenting her with this food in recognition of the fact that she was the real owner of the land upon which the house stood.

Kūmara
The sweet potato

This plant was subtropical in its origins and could be grown in Aotearoa only in the warmer and more fertile regions. Even there much skill and labour were required.

Since it was eaten on festive occasions and required a state of peace for its cultivation, the kūmara was symbolically associated with peace – in opposition to fernroot, which in many situations was associated with warfare.

Rongo, father of the kūmara, is generally regarded as one of the sons of Rangi and Papa, or sometimes as a son of Tāne. But this myth of origin does not tell us how human beings later acquired the kūmara. Each people possessed another myth that explained this.

Kupe
The explorer

The first person to visit Aotearoa was Kupe. When he arrived the land had not yet assumed its present form; Kupe established landmarks and prepared the way for the people who were to follow. According to one story, he overtook the land as it was floating along on the ocean; the ground was soft and trembling, and his first task was to make it firm and stationary. Some say he cut Aotearoa off from Hawaiki, to which it was then joined.

Often Kupe was believed to have cut the strait which separates the North and South Islands, forming as he did so numerous landmarks –

among them Kapiti, Māna and Arapawa Islands – which still bear witness to this exploit. In one story, he came to Aotearoa in pursuit of a giant octopus and finally killed it in this region.

He sailed around many coastal regions, especially the west coast of the North Island, and left behind possessions turned to stone, such as his sail, bailer and dogs. When his task was completed he returned to Hawaiki.

Kurahaupō
A waka claimed by many

In most of the traditions about waka that sailed from the homeland of Hawaiki to Aotearoa, the people who trace descent from them live in a single region. The *Kurahaupō*, however, is claimed by peoples in different parts of the country.

In the Far North, the peoples of Te Aupōuri and Te Rārawa say its captain was Pō and that the vessel is now a reef at Kapo-wairua (Spirits Bay).

On the west coast, the Taranaki people living near Mount Taranaki believe that in Hawaiki the *Kurahoupō* (as they call it) was broken by enemy sorcery, and that its owners, led by Te Mounga-roa and Turu, then accepted an invitation to sail to Aotearoa on the *Mātaatua*.

The historians of the *Aotea* acknowledge that the *Kurahaupō* was wrecked but claim that its captain was Ruatea and that he and his crew then joined their vessel, not the *Mātaatua*.

In the southern part of the North Island, in the coastal regions from the Whanganui River district to Hawke's Bay, a number of peoples claim descent from *Kurahaupō*. They believe that its captain was Whātonga and that it landed at Te Māhia [the Māhia Peninsula].

Lightning and thunder
Messages from the sky

In every district there is a hill or mountain where lightning used to warn the local people of a coming event. These hills are known as rua kōhā or rua kanapu. When lightning appeared on such a hilltop, or thunder was heard among their 'rumbling mountains' [maunga haruru], the people sought to discover the meaning of the omen.

Lightning is spoken of as supernatural fire [ahi tipua]. Many different kinds were recognised. Among the best known in some regions were Hine-te-uira [Lightning woman], who is sheet lightning, and Tama-te-uira [Lightning man], forked lightning.

Thunder in general is known as whaitiri, and was often associated with the mythical Whaitiri. But again there were numerous kinds of thunder, each with its own origin, name and significance.

Maero
Wild people

These savage, hairy people had long bony fingers and speared their prey with jagged nails. They ate their food raw, like fairies [patupaiarehe], but unlike fairies they were often solitary beings. While fairies could be danger-ous, maero were especially feared. They kidnapped men and women and would fight to the death.

They inhabited the great forests in the rugged interior of Taranaki and Whanganui, to which they had retreated when human beings arrived from Hawaiki and desecrated the tapu of their homes. In the hills and mountains of the South Island, where they were numerous, they were known as māeroero.

Māhaki
A Tūranga ancestor

The people known as Te Aitanga-a-Māhaki [The descendants of Māhaki] trace their origin to this early ancestor, a famous warrior who lived at Tūranga (the Gisborne district). His mother, Tauhei-kurī, was a daughter of Kahungunu. His father, Tama-taipū-noa, was from Ōpōtiki.

Māhaki-rau
Origin of the kahikatea

When Pou, having visited Hawaiki, was flying back to Aotearoa seated upon a bird lent him by Tāne, he pulled some feathers from under the bird's wings and threw them into the ocean. Under the water the feathers turned into a kahikatea tree which is still down there now, bearing fruit.

Later a branch from the tree came ashore. Some say it was washed up on the beach, others that a man named Māhaki-rau had a tame shark, Ika-hoea, which used to bring him fish when he was out on the ocean. To test the story of the underwater tree, Māhaki told his shark to fetch a branch; the shark did so, and Māhaki planted it. The branch grew into a tree, then a forest.

Māhanga
Reckless disregard for property

Māhanga was a man who readily abandoned his assets. The stories about him differ, but are always associated with a proverb that was quoted when someone was behaving as he was thought to have done. Of such a person it would be said, 'He's a descendant of Māhanga, who abandoned food and waka' [Te uri o Māhanga whakarere kai, whakarere waka].

In the Waikato district, Ngāti Māhanga associate the saying with their founding ancestor Māhanga, son of Tūheitia. Among the people of Tūhoe, Māhanga was a son of the early ancestor Tāne-atua. Others again used the proverb without reference to any particular ancestor.

Mahina
Discovered treasure

In the traditions of both *Tainui* and *Te Arawa* the crews of these waka, as they are about to make landfall at Whangaparāoa, see on the cliffs the scarlet flowers of pōhutukawa or rātā trees. One of the men believes them to be red plumes and thinks that in this new land such treasures are lying around everywhere. So he throws into the sea the red plumes he has brought from Hawaiki – and by the time he discovers his mistake, the real treasures have floated away.

The plumes are washed up on the beach and are found by Mahina, who keeps them. When asked to give them back, he replies, 'This is Mahina's treasure that's been washed up' [Ko te kura pae a Mahina]. These words are now a saying, equivalent to 'Finders keepers.' If the previous owner wants his possession back, he will have to pay.

Māhu
An ancestor in the Urewera

Māhu, a man of mysterious origins, lived in the early days in the Urewera Mountains with his wives and children. One day he sent six of his children for water, but they brought it from his tapu spring instead of the common one. In his rage he turned them into great round boulders, Te Whānau-a-Māhu [Māhu's family], which lie there still.

He then told his daughter Haumapūhia to draw water from the common spring, but she refused to go. He attempted to drown her, but she turned into a taniwha. She struggled and tunnelled, forming hollows and channels, until she had created Lake Waikaremoana. Then she became a rock, a tipua still to be seen there.

Māhu and Taewa
The acquisition of sorcery

Māhu lived long ago at Nukutaurua on Te Māhia (Māhia Peninsula). He and his wife were outraged one day when thieves stole kūmara from their storehouse, and Māhu determined to destroy the thieves through sorcery. To acquire the necessary knowledge he set out to visit Taewa-a-rangi, a powerful sorcerer who was married to his sister Mawake-roa. These two were living near Porangahau.

When Māhu reached their home, Taewa taught him the ritual chants that destroy human beings. Then Māhu did what was usual in these circumstances: he first directed his powers against a relative, his own flesh and blood. This relative was Kura-patiu, a daughter of Mawake-roa and Taewa. She turned to stone and she stands there still.

When Taewa's people came to mourn her, Māhu turned them all to stone as well; they can still be seen on a hillside. Then on his return to Nukutaurua he slew the men who had stolen his kūmara.

In Ngāti Kahungunu tradition, Māhu was held responsible for the acquisition of sorcery and all that happened as a consequence.

Māhuhu
Ancestral waka of Ngāti Whātua

Descent from *Māhuhu*, which arrived from the homeland of Hawaiki, is claimed especially by Ngāti Whātua in the Kaipara and Tāmaki regions, although peoples further north trace their origins to this waka as well.

Rongomai, captain of the *Māhuhu*, was drowned while fishing out at sea and his body was eaten by the trevally. For this reason the fish became tapu. In pre-Christian times none of his descendants would eat it.

Mahuika
Origin of fire

The trickster Māui acquired or invented many things necessary for human existence. Among them was fire, which he took from his grandmother (some say grandfather), Mahuika. Māui's family had not known how to kindle fire, and had been given it when necessary by Mahuika. But Māui tricked his grandmother into parting with all her fire, and from this time humans were in control of it.

This old woman's body, arms, legs, head and hair were full of fire. She offered Māui her little finger and he went away with it, but when he came to a stream he put out the fire, then went back and told her he had fallen in the water. So she gave him another finger, and he did the same thing again; he kept on like this until all her fingers were gone, and all but one of her toes.

Mahuika realised she had been tricked and flew into a rage. Pulling out the last toe she flung it on the ground, and the trees blazed up. Māui nearly died in the flames and smoke. But he called to his brothers, they sent heavy rain, and Mahuika's fire was overcome at last.

The old woman gathered up the remnants of her fire and placed them for protection in the kaikōmako tree. That is why fire can be kindled from fire-ploughs of kaikōmako wood. With such an instrument a skilled operator can produce a blazing fire in a few minutes.

Māhunui
The South Island

In the south they say that when Māui fished up Te Ika a Māui (the North Island), his waka the *Māhunui* became the South Island – which is consequently the older of the two. Māhunui is therefore a poetic, classical name for the South Island. Another name is Te Waka-a-Māui [Māui's waka].

Māhutonga
The Southern Cross

This group of stars is always moving around the southern sky. Ice, snow and frost live upon its summit, along with Pārāwera-nui, the south wind. A tohunga wishing to make the south wind blow would 'pull out the plug of Māhutonga so that great Pārāwera could come forth'.

Māia
Origin of the gourd

Gourds were grown for use as containers, and the immature fruit were a favourite vegetable. On the East Coast their origin was often attributed to Māia, who brought them from Hawaiki and initiated the rituals and practices associated with their cultivation.

In the Waiapu Valley, the belief was that Māia came to Aotearoa to escape from the great Uenuku, whom he had insulted. Uenuku was Māia's brother-in-law, being married to his sister, Te Rangatoro, and she now warned Māia to leave at once. She advised him to travel across the ocean inside a gourd with special powers, known as Te Ika-roa-a-Rauru [Rauru's long fish], and she gave him gourd seeds and told him how to grow them.

So Māia entered Te Ika-roa-a-Rauru and went bobbing along on the crests of the waves; a potent chant ensured his safe passage. He came ashore at Tūranga-nui (the Gisborne district), planted his seeds and looked after them carefully.

In Tūranga itself, some believe Māia arrived on a raft of gourds and others that he captained an ordinary waka, *Te Ika-roa-a-Rauru*, in this way bringing seeds of the gourd and knowledge of its cultivation.

Makawe
A guardian god

The village of Ōhinemutu on Lake Rotorua belongs to Ngāti Whakaue, one of the peoples of Te Arawa. On Pukeroa, the hill above, there stood the tūāhu of Makawe, for many generations their main atua. On the place where this shrine was located there is now a commemorative rock within an enclosure.

Māmari
A northern waka

This vessel sailed from the homeland of Hawaiki to the Hokianga Harbour. Some say it was captained by Nuku-tāwhiti and that his brother-in-law Rūānui accompanied him. Others believe that Rūānui captained the *Māmari* while Nuku-tāwhiti came on a different vessel.

People living further south, however, maintain that *Māmari* later sailed down the west coast and was wrecked near the beach at Riripo, just beyond the Maunganui Bluff. It lies there now, turned into a reef, at Ōmāmari [The place of *Māmari*].

Mana
Inherent power

This word mana can usually be defined as 'authority, influence, prestige, power, psychic force'. Traditionally, men and women who possessed mana had received it from their ancestors, both recent and early ones. It was not something that tūtūā [low-born people] could possess.

The mana of a rangatira could, however, increase or be lost. If the person failed to observe the rules of tapu required by their position, this would anger their atua and so endanger their mana. Incompetence as a leader would weaken their mana, while successful leadership, a proper self-respect, good fortune and skill in important undertakings would increase it.

A people collectively possessed mana, and again this could be lost, in battle or in other ways. But it was not only human beings who possessed mana. Any resource or important entity possessed its own mana.

In many circumstances, mana had to be protected by being entrusted to a guardian. A powerful rangatira might possess (and be responsible for) the mana of his people, and the mana of their land as well; his mana would ensure the safety of these other mana.

As well as human guardians of mana there were supernatural ones. The mana of a kūmara plantation, for instance, might be ritually conveyed to Rongo (who might be present in a stone figure termed a mauri). Rongo would then assume responsibility for the crop by transferring his own mana to the field. In effect, these two mana became one.

Manaia
An enemy three times defeated

The powerful tohunga Ngātoro-i-rangi, who came from Hawaiki on *Te Arawa*, was living peacefully at Maketū when he discovered that his brother-in-law Manaia, back in Hawaiki, was attempting to destroy him. So Ngātoro and his fellow tohunga, with seven-score warriors, set sail in the *Tōtara-i-karia* and soon reached Hawaiki.

Knowing that Manaia and his tohunga would proceed at dawn to their tūāhu, Ngātoro decided that his warriors would pretend to have been overcome by their sorcery. Following his instructions, his men hit themselves on the nose, smeared blood over their bodies and lay stiff as corpses in ritual ovens by the tūāhu.

Next morning their enemies shouted with delight when they saw the bloodied bodies stretched out in the ovens, apparently brought by their gods. Then Ngātoro's tohunga rushed from their place of concealment and slew Manaia's tohunga, while the warriors rose from the ovens and fought Manaia's men. All were killed, except Manaia himself. This great victory became known as Ihu-motomotokia [Thumped noses].

Ngātoro-i-rangi and his party then returned to their vessel, unaware that Manaia had fled and was already raising an army. Before they reached their ship there was another battle, which became known as Tara-i-whenua-kura. Again Manaia survived.

Having gained revenge, Ngātoro-i-rangi and his men returned to Aotearoa. Afterwards Ngātoro and his wife went off to Mōtītī Island, near Tauranga. They lived on their own there, growing their kūmara.

And there one evening Manaia appeared again, out on the water with a fleet of ships. When he shouted his challenge, Ngātoro replied that it was too dark to fight and that he should anchor his vessels and they would fight next day. Manaia agreed to this.

Meanwhile Ngātoro was reciting chants at his tūāhu. He called upon Tāwhirimātea to destroy his enemies, and Tāwhirimātea sent a great storm. There were shrieks and groans, then silence. When the old woman went out next morning she found the bodies lying on the beach. This defeat became known as Maikuku-tea [Whitened fingernails] because all that remained were bones and fingernails. Manaia, among the dead, was recognised by a tattoo on part of his hand.

These three battles, especially Ihu-motomotokia and Maikuku-tea, set precedents for overwhelming defeats in later times. They were recalled by orators and poets when prophesying disaster for enemies, or when lamenting and dignifying their own peoples' defeats.

Manaia
A family turned to rocks

The bold peak of Mount Manaia, part of the Whāngārei Heads, is sometimes said to have been one of a group of hills that arrived one night from their home across the western ocean. Another belief is that Manaia is a rangatira who arrived from Hawaiki with his family in the early times, then turned to stone. He and his wife, his daughters, his slave and his dog are now jagged rocks on the skyline.

Mangamangai-atua
Singing spirits

Some said that every utterance of these atua, their speech, laughter and shouting, took the form of ritual chants, ancient ones that cannot now be understood; others, however, heard the Mangamangai-atua singing songs that were perfectly intelligible. The quivering of the air on hot summer days was caused by the Mangamangai-atua as they danced and sang in the sky.

Mangapuera
A taniwha on the Whanganui

Some twenty generations ago this taniwha made his lair in a cave by the Ahuahu Stream, a tributary of the Whanganui. He was four metres long and two metres tall, with a scaly skin, shark teeth, bat wings, forelegs with claws, hindquarters with webbed feet, and a row of spines from head to tail. Unlike many taniwha he had no association with the local people, and he preyed upon men and women he found in the forest. Soon they fled the region and their pā lay deserted.

Then Tarawhiti, a man from Waitōtara, visited the district. He knew nothing about Mangapuera until he heard the taniwha crashing towards him. It was too late to run, so he climbed a tree, and as Mangapuera reached up he chopped off one of its forelegs with his adze. The other foreleg came up, and he chopped that off as well.

The infuriated creature lashed out with his tail, sweeping both tree and man to the ground, but he misjudged his strength and brought away the whole hillside. Caught in this landslide, the wounded taniwha moved slowly to extricate himself. Tarawhiti got out more quickly and dealt him a final blow.

Mangarara
An ancestral waka of Ngāti Porou

Sailing westward from Hawaiki, *Mangarara* came first to Whanga-o-keno (East Island), a small island by East Cape. The waka brought a cargo of tuatara and geckos, wētā and other insects, also two kinds of birds, pipits and oystercatchers. The ship's captain, Wheketoro, liberated his pets on the island, then to protect them he made the island tapu.

Wheketoro and his companions then set out for the mainland, but their ship was wrecked by a dog with extraordinary powers, named Moho-rangi; when this dog and its owner Tarawhata were thrown over-board, the dog kicked so hard that the vessel overturned. It was washed ashore and it turned to stone, while the crew settled in the region and became ancestors of Ngāti Porou.

Much later, a man named Kaiawa was living in Tūranga (the Gisborne district). He heard how abundant the kahawai were at Wharekāhika (Hicks Bay), and he made the journey north to see this sight. On the way he visited Ōpure, near Whanga-o-keno, where the rangatira was Tangaroa-hau.

This man wanted Kaiawa as a son-in-law, so he told him the fish were just as plentiful in this region. As proof he pointed to Whanga-o-keno, without mentioning that the island was tapu and could not be fished. So Kaiawa settled there and married Tangaroa-hau's daughter Whatumori. In time they had two daughters.

After some years, Kaiawa decided to remove the tapu from the island. The local people encouraged him in this dangerous task and he set out with his elder daughter, Pōnuiahine, whose assistance would be required in kindling the ritual fire.

At Whanga-o-keno they saw Tarawhata's dog, Mohorangi, which now took the form of a cliff. And they made a mistake, because Pōnuiahine's eyes should have been shaded to avoid the dog's intensely tapu gaze. As it was, the dog fixed his eyes upon her.

Kaiawa kindled a tapu fire with his daughter, then taking this fire he went to destroy Wheketoro's tapu. But on his return he found that Pōnuiahine had been turned to stone by Mohorangi. All he could do was weep.

Although Kaiawa had removed the tapu, he had paid a price. As a woman, Pōnuiahine possessed the powers necessary for the ritual creation of fire but she could not withstand the gaze of the Mohorangi.

Mango-huruhuru
Sands brought from Hawaiki

Long ago a tohunga named Mango-huruhuru, on the east coast of Te Wai Pounamu (the South Island), was visited by Pōtiki-roa, who had come from Taranaki seeking greenstone. Pōtiki-roa fell in love with one of the tohunga's daughters, Puna-te-rito, and he married her and for some years lived there with her people. Then he grew homesick and persuaded his father-in-law to accompany him to Taranaki.

At Waitaha (just south of Cape Egmont), the party were welcomed by Pōtiki-roa's relatives. Mango-huruhuru and his people built a large house on low land near the sea, while Pōtiki-roa lived with his wife on higher ground further inland.

The stony shore made it difficult to land their waka, so Mango-huruhuru decided to use his powers to solve this problem. Soon after sunset the old tohunga climbed to the ridgepole of his house, faced out to sea, and recited a long chant asking Papa the earth and Tangaroa in the ocean to send sand from the homeland of Hawaiki.

A dark cloud appeared on the horizon and rapidly advanced; it was a great storm bringing sand. By the end of the chant it had reached the people assembled on the shore. Soon they were buried, then the house as well. Mango-huruhuru's young daughter Heihana was turned to stone, and stands there now as proof of this story.

Pōtiki-roa and Puna-te-rito, in their house further inland, were the only survivors. The stone foundations of their house can be seen to this day.

Maniapoto
Founder of Ngāti Maniapoto

A rangatira generally had a principal wife and several secondary wives. Usually he married his principal wife first so that her children, as well as being high-born, would have the further advantage of primogeniture. This simplified questions of succession.

But Rereahu, eldest son of Raukawa, first took a wife who was not of high rank. Only many years later, when her children had grown up, did he marry another woman, the high-born Hine-au-pounamu. With her he had Maniapoto, then seven other children.

When Rereahu was on his death-bed he had to decide which son would inherit his mana. The choice lay between Te Ihingārangi, eldest son of his first wife, and Maniapoto. Although Te Ihingārangi was much older, Rereahu chose Maniapoto because of his rank and ability. This led to trouble between the brothers. In the end Maniapoto fought the jealous Te Ihingārangi, conquered him, and spared his life.

Maniapoto's descendants include the people of Ngāti Maniapoto, who belong to the Waipā Valley and the region south to the Mokau River.

Marakihau
Carved figures of taniwha

In some parts of the country, especially the southern Bay of Plenty and the Urewera, taniwha are depicted in meeting-houses as marakihau, creatures that have fish-like bodies below the waist, and heads rather like those of humans but with long hollow tongues. They are said use these tongues to suck down fish, and sometimes people and waka.

Yet taniwha in the ocean were usually said to take the form of whales, or sometimes sharks; there are few if any recorded stories concerning taniwha with hollow tongues. It seems that the word marakihau generally refers to carvings depicting taniwha rather than the creatures themselves.

Mārere-o-tonga
A source of knowledge

In some traditions this man and his companion, Takataka-pūtea, are a source of religious knowledge. Tūhoe people associate Mārere-o-tonga and Takataka-pūtea with knowledge of a different kind, regarding them as the originators of games and amusements such as dancing, playing musical instruments and storytelling. In some Arawa traditions they are twin sons of Rangi the sky and Papa the earth.

Maru
A fierce god

In the Rotorua region, Maru was a powerful atua whose protection was sought in times of war. His full name was Maru-te-whare-aitu [Maru the house of disaster]. There were tūāhu dedicated to him in different settlements, each with an intensely tapu symbol inhabited by the god.

On the west coast from Whanganui to northern Taranaki, Maru had other roles as well. At Whanganui he was described as the greatest of the gods. If a person had broken tapu and was about to die as a consequence, Maru might relent and save him if the appropriate chant was recited.

Maruiwi
A disastrous journey

When the Maruiwi people were forced to leave their homes at Waimana, inland from Ōhiwa in the southern Bay of Plenty, they decided to migrate to Heretaunga (Hawke's Bay) through the Taupō region. While on this journey, travelling secretly by night through rugged country north of Heretaunga, their party came to a great chasm. They did not see it in the darkness and they fell in one by one, first the leaders then those behind. Only seven survivors reached Heretaunga.

Orators and poets recall this occurrence when speaking of any people who have been destroyed, or may be in the future.

Maru-tūahu
Founder of Ngāti Maru

Maru-tūahu's father was Hotunui, an ancestor sometimes believed to have come on the *Tainui* but often said to be a son of Uenuku-tuwhatu. While living at Kāwhia, Hotunui was accused of the theft of some kūmara, and because of this insult he abandoned his home and his wife, Mihi-rāwhiti, who was pregnant at the time. He crossed the ranges to the Hauraki Gulf, settled at Whakatīwai among the people of Ngāti Pou, and married the sister of a rangatira named Te Whatu. Presently they had a son.

Meanwhile Mihi-rāwhiti, back at Kāwhia, also had a son. Following Hotunui's instructions she called the boy Maru-tūahu. When Maru grew up, he set out with a servant to find his father. After travelling for a month the two men reached the forests near Hotunui's home.

While Maru was up in a tree spearing tūī, and his servant was on the ground beneath, it happened that the two daughters of Te Whatu approached them. The younger sister was the first to see Maru in the tree, and she claimed him as her husband. So then the two women argued about him, because he was a fine-looking man.

At the village Maru was greeted by his father, Hotunui. And late that night Te Whatu's younger daughter went to Maru, and they slept together; by the time the elder sister found out, it was too late. So Maru-tūahu married Te Whatu's younger daughter and they became the founding ancestors of Ngāti Maru.

Maru and Hotunui went on living among Ngāti Pou, but Hotunui was insulted by the local people and this led to fighting. In the end Maru-tūahu and his men took possession of that place. His descendants continued to live there.

Mataaho
The overturning of the earth

A giant, Mataaho, is often held responsible, along with Rūaumoko, for earthquakes and volcanic activity. Some authorities trace the origin of these disturbances to a time long ago when Mataaho turned his mother Papa, the earth, face downwards so that she would no longer be made unhappy by the sight of Rangi the sky, from whom she was separated.

Mātaatua
Landfall at Whakatāne

Among the leading men who sailed from Hawaiki on the *Mātaatua* were the captain, Tōroa, and his brothers Puhi and Tāne-atua. The women included Tōroa's sister Muriwai and his daughter Wairaka.

When the waka landed at Whakatāne, only its stern was brought up on the shore. Next morning the waves were washing over the vessel and Wairaka called a warning. But the men were intent upon exploring their new land and they paid no attention. Wairaka had to secure the waka herself, having first remarked, 'Oh, I must make myself a man!' [Ē, kia whakatāne ake au i ahau!] This, it is said, is how Whakatāne gained its name.

Still preoccupied with exploration, Tōroa forgot to perform the ritual to mark their safe arrival; Muriwai had to do this herself, though it was wrong for a woman to do so. Back in Hawaiki their mother Wairakewa sensed something was amiss and set out for Whakatāne, seated on the trunk of a mānuka tree.

Tōroa and many of his family remained at Whakatāne, but Puhi sailed north with others. Tāne-atua explored the interior.

The peoples who trace descent to *Mātaatua* include Ngāti Awa, Te Whakatōhea and Tūhoe in the southern Bay of Plenty and the interior, Ngāi Te Rangi in Tauranga, and Ngā Puhi and Te Rārawa in the Far North. Some say it was Muriwai, not Wairaka, who saved the vessel and spoke the words that gave Whakatāne its name.

Matakauri
A giant-killer

Lake Wakatipu in the South Island had its origin in the death of a giant, Matau. When this monster carried off a woman named Manata, the daughter of a rangatira, the broken-hearted father promised her in marriage to any man who could rescue her.

A brave warrior named Matakauri determined to do so. He waited for a hot north-west wind, knowing Matau would be asleep at this time, then he armed himself and set out. Towards evening he found Manata. She told him, sobbing bitterly, that her captor had tied her to him with a long cord that could not be cut, because it was plaited from the hide of one of his ferocious two-headed dogs.

Nevertheless Matakauri went to a river and built a raft to carry her away. When all was ready and they still could not cut the cord, she wept all the more; her tears fell upon the cord and it parted at once. Matakauri's raft took them to safety and soon they were married.

The next time there was a north-west wind, Matakauri returned to kill Matau. He climbed the hill where the giant lay sleeping, piled bracken around him and set it on fire. The monster was burnt to death, and the fire burnt a deep hole in the ground in the shape of his body. Rivers filled this hole with water, forming Lake Wakatipu.

Matamata
A taniwha near Kaikōura

Just north of Kaikōura there was a place where the only track along the coast passed limestone bluffs. Late in the seventeenth century, when Ngāi Tahu were invading the South Island, Ngāti Māmoe at Kaikōura attempted to protect themselves by stationing their taniwha, Matamata, at the mouth of a stream there (its English name is Lyell Creek).

Matamata, a vicious-looking creature with a long neck and scaly body, for some time killed and devoured all the Ngāi Tahu warriors who came along the track. Eventually, however, he was overcome by a Ngāi Tahu rangatira named Maru.

Mataoho
Cause of Tāmaki's volcanoes

In Tāmaki (Auckland) the ancestor responsible for volcanic activity is usually said to be Mataoho, though sometimes his name is given as Mataaho. This giant felt cold one day and asked his gods to send fires to warm him. The gods made a vigorous response, forming the sixty or so volcanic hills and basins that now exist in the region.

The large crater of Maunga-whau (Mount Eden) is known as Te Ipu-a-Mataoho [Mataoho's bowl] and was sacred to him.

Mataora and Niwareka
Originators of tattooing and weaving

Niwareka was beaten by her husband, Mataora, and ran down to her father Uetonga in the underworld. Mataora followed, and Kūwatawata showed him the way.

In the underworld Mataora came to a place where Uetonga was tattooing a man. When Uetonga saw the designs painted on Mataora's face he wiped them off, saying, 'The people up there cannot tattoo properly.'

Then Mataora was thrown down and Uetonga began to tattoo him. When he felt the pain, Mataora sang a song to Niwareka. She heard this in the house where she sat weaving, and she left her work and came to him. She took him to her house and cared for him until his wounds had healed.

He told her then that they must go back to the world. They reached Kūwatawata's house and passed through safely, but when Mataora failed to give one of Niwareka's garments in payment, Kūwatawata called, 'Farewell, Mataora! The path to Night and the path to Day are now shut off, and living men will no longer pass over them.'

Afterwards Mataora lived with his wife in the world and taught people the art of tattooing. Niwareka, it is sometimes said, taught weaving.

Matariki
Stars bringing the new year

The English name for this small cluster of stars is the Pleiades; the Māori name, Matariki, means Little-eyes, or Little-points. In many parts of Aotearoa their appearance at dawn (or sometimes the first new moon after their appearance) marked the end of the old year and the beginning of the new. Generally seven stars were discerned.

Matariki is usually a woman. The seven stars were often regarded as Matariki and her six daughters, though others considered the entire group to be a single female.

Matariki's reappearance was greeted with songs lamenting the loss of those who had died in the previous year. But the singers' tears were joyful too, because the new year had begun.

Mataterā and Waerotā
Distant lands of origin

According to a tradition in the Far North, people migrated to Aotea (the North Island) from the islands of Mataterā, Waerotā and Hawaiki. These were lands of plenty where the kūmara grew wild, and abundant food was available without toil. But the people became numerous, there was fighting, and the ancestors set out to find a new home for themselves.

Of these mythic islands, Hawaiki is most often spoken of in tradition. However an East Coast harvest chant refers to Mataterā, and a northern lament speaks of Mataterā and Waerotā as lands to which the wairua of the dead make their way.

Matuatonga
A fertility god

On Mokoia Island in Lake Rotorua, an ancient stone figure known as Matuatonga was the dwelling place of an atua of this name who was believed to possess the power to ensure the fertility and abundance of the kūmara crop. Before the fields were planted each year the peoples in the region sent some of their seed kūmara across to the island. These kūmara were taken to the tūāhu and ceremonially brought into contact with

Matuatonga, while chants were recited to ensure a bountiful harvest. Most of the tubers then returned to their owners, conveying with them the mana of Matuatonga, while a few were ritually presented to Matuatonga to ensure his protection.

This ancient figure of Matuatonga is now in the Auckland Museum. But another figure of Matuatonga, apparently carved in the nineteenth century as a replacement, still stands upon the slopes of Mokoia.

Matuku-tangotango
Rata's enemy

This demonic being kills and devours Wahieroa, the father of Rata, and Rata accordingly sets out on a voyage to avenge his father's death. He succeeds in this undertaking, usually by catching Matuku-tangotango in a great noose. In some versions, this happens on a path near the monster's home. In other accounts, Matuku-tangotango lives underground and comes up only when there is a new moon, so Rata snares him at this time.

Māui
The trickster hero

This man comes early in the genealogies, at a point where the world and its inhabitants have been formed but human beings still lack many of the things they need. Māui shapes the environment further, provides important resources for humans and demonstrates useful skills.

He himself is very much a human being, despite his extraordinary powers. He achieves his ends through trickery, very often, and by breaking the rules. He performs no feats of arms, concerns himself with practical, domestic matters, and tends to do things the 'wrong,' non-prestigious way. Much of his power, it seems, comes from breaking tapu.

There is first the manner of his birth; he is a miscarried foetus that survives and grows in the sea (or some other unpromising environment). In Māori belief, an aborted foetus or stillborn infant might turn into a spirit of an especially dangerous kind (atua kahukahu). Māui himself is not such a spirit; he miraculously survives and is finally accepted into his kinship group. Nevertheless the resemblance is there, and makes for ambiguity. No wonder there is a recognition scene in which Māui persuades his mother Taranga, with difficulty, that he is her son.

Māui is the youngest of five brothers – or some say four. (His full name is Māui-tikitiki-o-Taranga, and the others are variously known as Māui-mua, Māui-taha, Māui-roto, Māui-waho and Māui-pae.) Like many heroes in mythology he acts vigorously to overcome his low status as the youngest son.

There is also his name. Since a number of figures in Māori tradition (such as Tāne and Rangi) have names that suggest their nature, it must be significant that the word māui is the ordinary term for the left, and the left hand. This was the noa [profane, ordinary] side of the body, as opposed to the tapu [sacred] right side. Māui is not a personification as such, but this area of meaning is relevant to the way he behaves.

Māui's close relationship with his mother rather than his father is unusual in a hero. Wanting to know what Taranga does all day, he spies on her, then turns himself into a pigeon. He follows her down under the ground, and there is a second recognition scene between them.

In a well-known episode, Māui steals fire from Mahuika, tricking her by going back for more until all is gone. Māui's dramatic victory over Mahuika and her fire is a victory for all human beings.

The funniest trick may have been Māui's persuading his brother-in-law to let him tattoo him and then – with Irawaru at his mercy, and with the aid of a potent chant – pulling him out into the shape of a dog.

Māui also conquered the sun; he noosed it as it came up, reciting a chant that forced it to go more slowly. So now the days are long enough for the things people have to do.

His most spectacular exploit was fishing up the land. The North Island is Māui's Fish [Te Ika-a-Māui] and the South Island, according to its inhabitants, is the waka from which Māui caught his fish.

For a long time Māui was too lazy to go out fishing, then his wives shamed him into acquiring a fish hook. He did this his own way, by visiting the tapu cave that contained the bones of his grandparent, Muriranga-whenua; he took the jawbone and it became his hook. Normally only an enemy would use a human bone for this purpose, and then only if he intended the worst insult possible. Yet Māui was able to break tapu in this horrendous way without any ill effects. Indeed he gained great power by doing so.

His elder brothers did not want him in their waka, fearing his tricks, but he hid, then sprang up when out on the ocean. They anchored above the fishing rock and the elder brothers set to work, but they would not give Māui any bait. So he punched himself on the nose and used his own blood as bait, and a fish took his hook at once.

The waka was lifted up then down, it spun round, and his brothers cried out in fear. But Māui would not let go his fish. He recited a chant and the fish came up. Soon it stretched out upon the surface, the vessel high and dry on its back.

Māui went off to make offerings to the gods, telling his brothers to leave the fish alone until his return. But the greedy brothers began to chop it up. It was not yet dead, and it writhed into mountains, cliffs and gorges. That is why the lie of the land is now so bad.

The last episode in Māui's story is his encounter with Hine-nui-te-pō [Great woman the night]. Māui wanted to pass through Hine's body to kill her, and do away with death. He approached the great woman as she lay sleeping, he entered her body, she brought her legs together, and that was the end of him. He had tried once too often to reverse the normal order of things.

Mauri
Repositories of vitality

It was believed that a person, a people, a pā or house or waka, a river or forest, a food resource of any kind – any entity of value – possessed a life force, a vitality, which was termed a hau. In the case of a person, this hau was identified with the breath, and a number of bodily states involving the breath (such as being startled, or sneezing) were said to be the act of the person's mauri. With a person, then, the hau and the mauri were both located within the body.

With other entities they were closely related but in a different way. In these other cases, the hau was strengthened and protected from enemies by being ritually located within a material counterpart, usually a stone, which was termed a mauri. At the same time a protective atua, sometimes more than one, was located in the stone as well.

In this way the mauri served to bring together the vitality [hau] of the entity, and a guardian spirit. If the mauri was kept safe, all would be well with the people, resource, or other entity with which it was identified.

Miru
Ruler of Night

In a Taranaki tradition, Miru lives in the underworld in a house known as Te Tatau o Te Pō [The door to night]. His companions are atua that afflict human beings with illness and misfortune, and are involved in sorcery. Miru himself possesses much knowledge of history, ritual chants and sorcery.

Two men in Hawaiki, Ihenga and Rongomai, lead an expedition to visit him. They climb down a rope, are invited into Miru's house and remain there for many days and nights, acquiring knowledge. But Miru's manner changes and the men become suspicious. When they rush from the house, Miru seizes two laggards, Ngo and Kewa, and keeps them as payment for the knowledge he has imparted.

The travellers soon find that their rope has been cut. Then they see that Ngo and Kewa are missing. They return, but Miru will not give up his two captives and finally kills them. Ihenga and his companions then plan their revenge. While Miru and his attendant spirits are asleep in their house they set it on fire, and its occupants are burnt to ashes.

Only with great difficulty, after a dangerous voyage, do the survivors of the expedition return to their home in Hawaiki.

Moa
Extraordinary birds

Eleven species of moa once browsed on trees and shrubs in Aotearoa, being especially common in the eastern part of the South Island. The tallest of these wingless birds were 2.5 metres (8 feet) in height, and the heaviest weighed more than 200 kilograms (440 pounds). When the first settlers arrived about a thousand years ago, they called these new birds by the same name as the domestic fowls [moa] they had left behind in their previous home.

The presence of these huge birds, along with smaller species of flightless birds and numerous colonies of seals, must have led to a rapid increase in the population. As a result, the moa did not last very long. Moa-hunting reached its peak in about 1300; great numbers were killed in the century that followed, by 1500 they had become rare, and soon afterwards they disappeared completely.

A common expression, 'lost like the moa' [mate-ā-moa], means 'lost utterly and hopelessly'. As well, moa appear in tradition as remote creatures with extraordinary attributes which live on the summits of certain mountains.

Moeahu
A dog-headed man

This fierce creature was like a man except for his dog's head and feet. He howled, but had human intelligence. He could run very fast and no man could escape him. His weapons were a taiaha and a whalebone patu, and as well he used his muzzle and feet. He lived with his brothers and sisters in a forest in the Tūranga (Gisborne) region.

A man named Te Kowha once stole some fish that Moeahu's people had left drying on a stage, and in retaliation Moeahu ate some preserved birds that belonged to Te Kowha. The man seized his spear, but the monster broke it; he fled, but was clubbed to the ground. When his three brothers ran to his assistance they were killed as well.

Moko-hiku-waru
A powerful reptile

In the Taranaki and Whanganui regions, Moko-hiku-waru is a powerful reptile god that is often linked with a similar god named Tū-tangata-kino. These two reptiles guarded the house of Miru, ruler of the underworld. They were very dangerous and might attack human beings, especially when employed in sorcery by knowledgeable persons. In some circumstances, though, humans could employ them as guardians.

Moko-ika-hiku-waru˙
An eight-tailed taniwha

In Tainui tradition, Moko-ika-hiku-waru is a taniwha in the form of an eight-tailed reptile. One of the taniwha that guided the *Tainui* on its voyage from Hawaiki, he left the ship at Tāmaki (the Auckland district), along with those of the crew who had decided to settle there. He made his home in a deep pool at the entrance to a lagoon (the Panmure Basin), and he fed upon the eels, flounder and yellow-eyed mullet that abounded there. For this reason these fish were tapu, never eaten by human beings.

Moko's Great Dog
A ferocious beast

The Ngāmoko Range borders the eastern shore of Lake Waikaremoana. Men who hunted birds on its precipitous slopes sometimes failed to return, and it was discovered that they had been devoured by a savage creature known as Moko's Great Dog [Te Kurī nui a Moko].

The warriors of Waikaremoana resolved to trap and kill this monster. They constructed a strong cage from saplings and vines, baited it with meat, cautiously placed it near the animal's den, then hid nearby. The dog scented the meat and entered the cage, the door was quickly shut, and the men speared the howling beast through the sides of the cage. Soon it lay dead.

The dog had no mate, so after this the bird-hunters were undisturbed. Sometimes they camped in the large cave where the monster had lived.

Monoa
Whiro's son, who escaped

In some traditions from the west coast of the North Island, a great house named Te Whare Kura [The crimson house] was erected at Hawaiki as a place in which to impart sacred knowledge. The rangatira who did this belonged to two great factions, and there was feuding between them.

When the house was completed, one of these factions sent a treacherous message inviting their enemy, the evil Whiro, to attend as a leading orator. Whiro told the messenger that two of his sons would go instead. So these young men entered Te Whare Kura, and were killed at once.

When other messengers were sent, Whiro again declined and said that Monoa, his remaining son, would go in his place. But he warned Monoa to make his way cautiously to the house, climb the roof and look down through the smoke-hole. When Monoa did this, he saw the hearts and lungs of his brothers being offered to the gods by the tohunga. He fled, and the men in the house pursued him.

Monoa ran into a flock of shags, then a flock of ducks, then godwits, oystercatchers and black-backed gulls, but none of these birds could hide him. Then he ran into a flock of terns – small birds that fly in large flocks – and he was completely hidden. His pursuers could not find him, so he escaped.

Moon
A return to life

All living beings beneath the moon will die, while those above will live forever. The fate of Te Marama [The moon] is different, because every month he dies, then comes back to life. He bathes in Tāne's living waters [Te Wai-ora-o-Tāne], and three nights later he is alive again.

Sayings and songs contrast this renewal with the fate of human beings.

Since people counted by nights of the moon rather than by days, the changing shape of this bright being served to measure time. For longer periods there were the months of the year, again regulated by the moon.

There is a woman in the moon, called Rona. He seized her and took her up when she rashly cursed him one dark night.

Motu-tapu
A sacred island

In a myth known throughout Polynesia, Hina (or Hine) hears about the handsome Tinirau and wants him as her husband. She swims through the ocean for many days to reach his island (which is often called Motu-tapu), she finds him there, marries him and has his son.

In Aotearoa, this woman is occasionally Hina but usually Hine-te-iwaiwa, and the story often takes place in Hawaiki or an unnamed land. However there is an island in this country which was known originally as Te Motu-tapu-a-Tinirau [Tinirau's sacred island]. It lies in the middle of Lake Rotorua and was, we are told, given this name by the explorer Īhenga. Later its name was changed to Mokoia.

The interesting thing is that while there is no story associating the mythical Hina or Hine with this island, a well known legend tells how an ancestor, Hinemoa, evaded her relatives and swam across Lake Rotorua to reach the island and marry Tūtānekai; again, all ends happily. Perhaps the legend of Hinemoa has been shaped by the ancient story of Hine, who swam bravely across the water to find the man she had made up her mind to marry.

Mountains
The high places

Every people had a special association with a hill or mountain of mana. Its tapu summit stood apart, a source and expression of the people's mana and their point of contact with the sky. Lightning and thunder brought messages concerning the future, and the bones of high-ranking people were often laid to rest in caves upon their mountains' heights.

The country is so mountainous because Māui's brothers ignored his instructions and hacked up his fish while it was still alive, so that it writhed into hills and ridges. Volcanoes were sometimes believed to have been caused by a giant named Mataaho, though others thought Rūaumoko responsible, and it was Ngātoro-i-rangi who had summoned from Hawaiki the volcanic fires and hot springs now to be seen in the territories of his descendants.

In the south, the men who came on the *Āraiteuru* arrived by night and spread out over the countryside, then turned into mountains when the sun rose. In some other places, the mountains themselves had moved around under cover of darkness then been transfixed by the light.

Traditionally, the name Tongariro belonged to the peaks that are known now as Tongariro, Ruapehu and Ngāuruhoe, since these three were then regarded as a single mountain. Tongariro lives where he has always done, but others separated from him and went in different directions. Two rounded hills, Pihanga and Hauhungatahi, are his wives, but they now stand at some distance. Another male, Taranaki, once lived with Tongariro, but they fought, some say over Pihanga, and Taranaki went rushing off in the darkness, digging with his great bulk the gorge of the Whanganui River. When the sun rose he was far in the west, and he has been there ever since.

Mumuhau and Takeretou
Two wise birds

The saddleback is a dark bird with a chestnut 'saddle' and orange wattles. Its cries were often taken to be good or bad omens, and it was believed to act as a guardian. Ancient buried treasures were sometimes thought to be protected by these birds.

The *Mātaatua*, while sailing from Hawaiki, was guarded and guided by two saddlebacks with extraordinary powers, Mumuhau and Takeretou. At the entrance to the Hauraki Gulf the crew placed these tipua on Repanga (Cuvier Island) and they are living there still.

Muturangi's Octopus
The monster killed by Kupe

In Hawaiki, or some say Rarotonga, a giant octopus, the pet of an ill-disposed tohunga named Muturangi, kept stealing the bait from Kupe's fishing lines. This creature is generally known as Muturangi's octopus [Te Wheke a Muturangi].

When Kupe angrily pursued the octopus, it sped across the ocean to Aotearoa. Kupe followed, and in Raukawa (Cook Strait) he fought the great creature, hacking at its arms. Then he threw overboard a bundle of gourds; the octopus attacked these, thinking them a person, and this gave Kupe the opportunity he needed.

After killing the octopus, Kupe placed its eyes upon a group of small rocky islands that henceforth became known as Ngā Whatu [The eyes]. (Their English name is The Brothers.) And because Ngā Whatu were very tapu, Kupe created a strong current in the ocean nearby to ensure that voyagers would respect their sacredness and stay well away.

Travellers did indeed observe great care in passing this dangerous place. They avoided meeting the gaze of Ngā Whatu, often by wearing eye-shades of leaves.

Ngahue
Owner of the greenstone fish

In Hawaiki, two people each had a pet fish consisting of stone: Ngahue's fish, named Poutini, was greenstone, while Hine-tua-hōanga's fish, Wai-apu, had a back of obsidian and a belly of flint. These people used to allow their pets to swim in the ocean, but Hine-tua-hōanga became jealous and wanted her fish to be the only one in the sea.

She drove Ngahue and his fish away from Hawaiki, pursuing them across the ocean and finding them at last on Tūhua (Mayor Island); when she threw part of her own fish on to this island, the greenstone fish became frightened and went swimming away across the ocean, with Ngahue still in pursuit. It swam to Arahura on the West Coast, and now lives in the rivers there.

Ngahue, however, returned home, taking part of his fish with him. From this greenstone he made adzes, tiki and ear pendants. The adzes, some say, were used subsequently in making the waka that brought the ancestors to Aotearoa.

Ngāi-te-heke-o-te-rangi
Taniwha at Kāwhia

This group of fifteen taniwha live near Te Māhoe, by the Waiharakeke inlet of the Kāwhia Harbour. One of them, Ngā-tara-tū, is a man-eater. The others are kindly disposed and sometimes save people from drowning.

Ngake
Kupe's companion

The early explorer Kupe is sometimes believed to have been accompanied by a companion, Ngake. It is said that when Kupe pursued Muturangi's octopus from Rarotonga to Raukawa (Cook Strait), he and his men sailed on *Mātāhorua* while Ngake and his men travelled on *Tawhiri-rangi*. At Raukawa they together fought and killed the octopus. They then explored Te Wai Pounamu (the South Island), discovering greenstone at Arahura.

Ngake is sometimes identified with Ngahue, owner of the greenstone fish.

Ngake and Whātaitai
Taniwha that formed a harbour

In the early times two taniwha, Ngake and Whātaitai, were confined within a great lake. Both tried to escape to the ocean by forcing a passage through the surrounding land; Whātaitai failed to do so, but Ngake succeeded in opened up a channel to the sea, thereby forming Te Whanga-nui-a-Tara (Wellington Harbour).

Whātaitai's struggles did, however, create the indentation now known as Evans Bay. As Hātaitai his name now belongs to a nearby suburb.

Ngātokowaru
A rangatira of Ngāti Raukawa

This warrior lived south of Mount Maungatautari in the early eighteenth century. After much military success, his army was defeated near Taupiri by Ngāti Mahuta. Ngātokowaru himself was taken prisoner by the son of the great rangatira Te Putu.

Knowing he would be killed, Ngātokowaru asked if he could first meet Te Putu. And as Te Putu – then an old man – bent forward courteously to hongi with him, Ngātokowaru pulled from his cloak a hidden dagger and stabbed him in the throat. He then quickly smeared himself with Te Putu's blood.

At once he was killed. But because of this contact with Te Putu's blood he escaped the victors' ovens, as he had known he would, and his bold action won him lasting fame.

Ngātoro-i-rangi
A great tohunga

This ancestor of the Arawa peoples was a tohunga with extraordinary powers. During the voyage of Te Arawa from Hawaiki he flew into a rage when the captain, Tama-te-kapua, stole his wife Kea-roa, and he sent the vessel towards the abyss at the edge of the ocean. Only at the last moment did he relent and bring it back up.

After the ship made landfall at Maketū, Ngātoro set out to explore the interior. At Taupō he encountered Tia, a relative who had come on Te

Arawa and was now seeking land for himself and his descendants. Ngātoro tricked Tia into believing he had a prior claim, so Tia left this region to Ngātoro and made his way to Tokaanu.

Ngātoro also met Hape, who belonged to one of the early peoples already established in the country. Realising that Hape was also looking for land, Ngātoro asserted his own claim by climbing the high peak of Tongariro (which is now known as Ngāuruhoe). Hape attempted the climb as well, but Ngatoro's gods sent a snowstorm that destroyed his rival.

When Ngātoro and his slave stood upon the summit they were benumbed with cold, so Ngātoro called to his sisters back in Hawaiki and asked for fire. The sisters, Te Pupū and Te Hoata, heard him and came at once. Their fire burns still in the crater of Ngāuruhoe, and in the many other places in Arawa territory where thermal and volcanic activity exists.

After his return to Maketū, Ngātoro still had before him a series of encounters with a brother-in-law, Manaia, who was trying to destroy him. In this contest of powers Ngātoro was triumphant.

Night
The darkness

In the beginning there was darkness. Some say the world began with the embraced sky and earth, others that generations of beings, or entities, first evolved and coupled. These had names, some of them, such as Te Pō Uriuri [Dark night] and Te Pō Tangotango [Black night]. Later came the sky and earth, then the light.

The eternal lights, the Sun by day and the Moon and stars by night, belong with Rangi the sky father. Darkness belongs with Papa the earth mother, for within her, or beneath, there is the underworld to which the wairua of the dead leap down. In this underworld there lives Hine-nui-te-pō [Great woman the night], the woman who brought death into the world. Night and the underworld were inseparably associated, both being known by the one expression, Te Pō [Night].

Since night belonged with Papa and Hine-nui-te-pō, females generally were associated with darkness – which had associations with defeat and death. Males, on the other hand, were associated with the light – which was associated with life and success. Yet the darkness had great power, as women in fact did. The world after all had come from darkness, just as new life came in fact from women, and it was darkness (and the woman

Hine-nui-te-pō) that received people at the end of their lives. The powers of darkness and of light were more evenly balanced in Māori thought and experience than a simplistic interpretation might suggest.

Nukumaitore's Descendants
An island of women

Two stories tell of an island populated by women known as Nukumaitore's descendants [Te Aitanga-a-Nukumaitore]. Sometimes there are men as well, but the emphasis is on the women's presence.

When Tura visits the island, he finds that the women make no use of fire. He teaches them how to kindle fire and cook in an oven, then he takes a wife and discovers that he must teach the proper methods of childbirth. In introducing this knowledge he establishes the procedures that humans have followed ever since.

In the other tale, two castaways, Pungarehu and Kōkōmuka, teach the islanders, who this time include men, how to kindle fire and cook. Then they show them how to kill a giant bird, Te Pouākai, which has been preying upon them. Afterwards they feel homesick and return to their own land.

Nuku-tawhiti and Rūānui
Ancestors of Ngā Puhi

Two ancestors, Nuku-tawhiti and Rūānui, are held mainly responsible for the settlement of the Hokianga region. The story begins with the explorer Kupe, who was there first. Some say Nuku-tawhiti met him in Hokianga, others that the meeting occurred back in Hawaiki and that Kupe, who had just returned from Hokianga, gave Nuku sailing directions and also his own ship, *Ngātokimātāwhaorua*. Rūānui meanwhile decided to accompany Nuku and made ready his vessel, the *Māmari*.

Arrived in Hokianga with their followers, the two rangatira set about building themselves carved houses. This made them rivals, because Rūānui finished his house first and would not wait so that both houses could be ceremonially opened at the same time. In a further demonstration of his mana, he summoned a whale to strand itself on the beach to provide meat for the feast that would accompany his opening ceremony.

Nuku-tawhiti created a sandbank and shut out the whale, but Rūānui called upon Tangaroa, ruler of the sea, and a great wave swept the whale over the sandbank and towards his house. In this way he defeated Nuku-tawhiti, despite his powers, and he never afterwards submitted to him.

The quarrel between the two men continued between their descendants and followers for some six generations. After this they began to intermarry.

These two rangatira are among the founding ancestors of Ngā Puhi. Rūānui is also an early ancestor of the peoples of Te Rārawa and Te Aupōuri.

Ocean
The surrounding waters

The ocean, like the earth, is female. In some regions, such as Whanganui and Heretaunga (Hawke's Bay), she is Hine-moana [Ocean woman]. In the southern Bay of Plenty she is Wainui [Great waters], one of the three children of Rangi and Papa. In the Tūranga (Gisborne) district her name is Moana-nui [Great ocean].

Owheao
A taniwha at Taupō

In the sixteenth century an ancient people known as Ngāti Hotu, occupants of the Taupō district, came under pressure from sections of Ngāti Tūwharetoa. The fighting continued for several generations, with Ngāti Tūwharetoa gradually establishing themselves in the region. Victory was finally assured when Tūrangi-tukua and other rangatira of Ngāti Tūwharetoa managed to destroy Owheao, the taniwha guardian of Ngāti Hotu. Strong ropes were plaited, a snare was set at the entrance to the taniwha's cave, and a young woman was sent as a decoy. Owheao emerged at once and was caught in the snare.

Pahiko
A voyage to Hawaiki

At Reporua on the East Coast the people of Te Wahine-iti (or Ngāti Pakura), a section of Ngāti Porou, were enslaved after losing a series of battles with the peoples around them. Their leader, Pahiko, determined to seek another home, and told his people to steal their masters' seed kūmara and cook and preserve them as food for the voyage. When all was ready, they sailed one night in a vessel belonging to their masters. They set their course towards the rising sun and sailed back to the homeland of Hawaiki. There they found their relatives who had stayed behind.

Paia
Tāne's assistant

In the beginning Tāne separated his father Rangi the sky from his mother Papa the earth so that their children would have room to move, and light could be seen. Mostly he is said to have performed this feat on his own, but some say he was helped by a brother, or sister, named Paia.

When Paia is a man, he is often said to possess ritual powers, but when Paia is a younger sister her role is to encourage Tāne to perform the deed. In a myth from Moeraki, Tāne and his sister Paia marry and produce the first human beings.

Others assert that Tāne and Paia-te-rangi are one and the same person.

Paikea
A journey on a whale

In Hawaiki, Paikea was one of seven-score sons of the great rangatira Uenuku. Another of these young men, Ruatapu, considered himself insulted by his father and determined to gain revenge by murdering his brothers. A new ship had been built, and the sons set out on its first voyage in ignorance of the fact that Ruatapu had bored a hole in the bilge and was covering it with his foot. Far out on the ocean he let the water rush in and the vessel capsized. Then Ruatapu drowned all his brothers except Paikea, who escaped.

Paikea recited a long chant, and a taniwha in the form of a whale came and carried him on his back. His journey ended at Ahuahu (Great Mercury Island) in Aotearoa. Thinking he was in Hawaiki, he walked south seeking his home. At Whakatāne he married a woman, Manawa-tina. But he was still homesick, so he abandoned his wife and children and continued on.

Near East Cape he met Huturangi, daughter of Whiro-nui and Ārai-awa. He married her, then soon moved on again, taking her with him. At last they reached a place on the coast which was very similar to Whāngārā-i-tawhiti [Whāngārā in the distance], Paikea's lost home. Paikea liked this place very much. He named it Whāngārā and spent the rest of his life there.

Paikea is one of the most important ancestors of Ngāti Porou. Some say he was the eldest of Uenuku's sons, and that until his journey his name was Kahutia-te-rangi.

Pane-iraira
A taniwha guardian

Some say Pane-iraira was one of the taniwha that guided the *Tainui* during its voyage from Hawaiki. Others claim that the tohunga Raka-taura made his way across the ocean seated upon his back.

Pane-iraira continued his association with the people of Tainui. When a vessel capsized at sea he sometimes carried the crew to safety. From time to time he would communicate with a tohunga possessed of special powers, and on the death of one of these men he would send a whale to strand itself, providing the best food for the funeral.

Pani
Mother of the kūmara

The main idea in this myth is that a woman, Pani, gave birth to the kūmara. The details vary. According to a Ngāti Awa authority, Hāmiora Pio, a man named Rongo-māui climbed to the sky to acquire the kūmara from his elder brother Whānui (the star Vega). Whānui would not part with the kūmara, but Rongo-māui stole it anyway and placed it in his penis. He then went back down to his wife, Pani-tinaku [Seed-kūmara Pani].

When Pani became pregnant, she told her husband to take her to the waters of Mona-ariki. There she recited a ritual chant and gave birth to her 'kūmara children' [tamariki kūmara], the many different varieties of kūmara. Rongo-māui then performed the rituals appropriate to the kūmara harvest, in this way setting the pattern for the future.

Pānia

A woman from the sea

Pānia's home was in the sea, but she used to spend the night near the entrance to the harbour at Ahuriri (Napier). One evening a young ranga-tira, Karitoki, discovered her there and made her his wife. After this she visited her husband every night, but always left at dawn. In time she gave birth to a son.

Thinking the boy might be taken away by the people of the sea, Karitoki asked a tohunga for his assistance. The tohunga told him to wait until his wife and son were asleep, then remove their tapu by placing cooked food upon them. When this was done they would not be able to return to the sea.

The husband did this, but perhaps the food was not properly cooked, because Pānia went back to her people and never returned. Her son Moremore became a taniwha, the guardian [kaitiaki] of the rich resources of seafood in the harbour.

Pānia is now a fishing rock. She can be seen, when the sea is calm, lying face downwards with her arms towards the shore. The fish in her left armpit are rock cod, those in her right armpit are snapper, and those between her thighs are hāpuku.

Paoa

A Hauraki ancestor

This founding ancestor of Ngāti Paoa came to Hauraki from the Waikato region. At Kaitotehe, by Taupiri Mountain, he married a high-ranking woman and had two sons, then deserted them and married a beautiful slave woman. The high-ranking woman lived alone with her sons, while Paoa lived some distance away with his new wife.

One day Paoa had no kūmara to offer some visitors, and in desper-ation he sent his new wife to beg for kūmara from his first wife. When she refused to help, he was overcome with shame. He abandoned his home and set out that very night for the Hauraki region. There he became the rangatira of the people of Mirimiri-rau, a pā on the Piako River.

His fame spread throughout Hauraki and finally reached Ruawhea, where the rangatira was Taharua. This man's daughter, Tukutuku, was well known for her industry and good management, and she was not yet married, having so far rejected all suitors. When a party from Paoa's pā visited Ruawhea, the young woman questioned them eagerly about him. She entertained her visitors lavishly, and on their return they told Pāoa about her.

So that autumn Paoa set out to visit Tukutuku. His party paddled down the Piako River and up the Waihou, and came at last to Ruawhea. At first Tukutuku was too shy to approach Paoa, but her parents encouraged her and soon they were married. On their return to Mirimirirau, Tukutuku's skills and generosity attracted many people around her.

In Paoa's old age he persuaded his Hauraki sons to take him to the Waikato to visit his sons there, whom he had not seen since his departure. They did so, but the encounter led to a fight in which the Waikato men were killed.

Papa
The first woman, the earth

Papa's name means Foundation, or Flat Surface. She is the earth that stretches out beneath her husband Rangi, the sky, and she is the first woman. The world came into being when Tāne separated Rangi and Papa, pushing Rangi upwards and allowing light to come between them.

Papa has a number of extended names, such as Papa-tūā-nuku [Widespread Papa]. She supports and sustains her human children, providing food and the other conditions necessary for life, yet inevitably she is inferior to her husband Rangi because she lies below that sacred realm, and Night [Te Pō] is within her. The earth is the house of Aituā [Misfortune], and her children enter her body when they die. The sky, on the other hand, is the house of life, because the persons who light it live forever.

As the primal parents, Rangi and Papa set the pattern for their descendants. Women were thought to take their nature from the first female: while men in general were sacred and set apart [tapu], women's nature was in general everyday, ordinary, profane [noa]. All this and much more was established in the beginning.

The geneologies that trace the history of the world begin with Rangi and Papa,then come down through the generations to the present day.

Papa-kauri
A tipua of Hauraki

This was a tipua, a supernatural being, who belonged to the Hauraki peoples and was their mauri, a source and symbol of their vitality and mana. He took the form of a stump of a kauri tree [papa-kauri], easily recognisable by the flax bush growing upon it.

When someone of Ngāti Maru was about to die, Papa-kauri left his resting place near the mouth of the Waihou River and moved out over the water. The direction of the tide made no difference; he kept moving outward.

Parawhenuamea
Rivers and streams

Parawhenuamea is generally regarded as the origin of the waters of the earth. She is the streams flowing from the mountains, and she is flood-waters, so it is not surprising that she is often regarded as a daughter of Tāne and Hine-tūpari-maunga [Mountain cliff woman]. Sometimes her husband is Kiwa, guardian of the ocean.

Pare and Hutu
The woman who was brought back

Pare was a great lady, as yet unmarried, who lived in a fine carved house surrounded by three fences. One day when her people were playing games, whipping tops and throwing darts, they were joined by an unknown rangatira. This man, Hutu, showed great skill, and the people applauded so loudly that Pare came to the door of her house. Hutu's dart landed by the door and Pare caught it up. When he went to fetch it, she asked him inside and said she loved him.

Hutu told her he already had a wife and children, Pare kept insisting, and in the end he ran off. So Pare, suffering from love and shame, ordered her attendants to adorn her house. Then when everything was ready she killed herself.

Pare's people said that Hutu must die for this. Hutu told them he was willing to die, but that first he must go to the underworld. He set off, reached Te Rēinga, and jumped down.

In the underworld, Pare was inside a house and would not come out. He showed the people how to throw darts and whip tops, but she did not respond. So he taught them to make a giant swing. They fastened ropes to a treetop, bent the tree to the ground, and Hutu sat upon it with someone on his shoulders. Then they let go the ropes and the tree sprang up.

The people were delighted, and made such a commotion that Pare's wairua came to watch. Soon she asked to sit on his shoulders. They pulled the tree down, then it sprang back with such force that the ropes flew up to the land above. Hutu kept climbing up with Pare on his shoulders, and at last they reached the upper world. When Pare's wairua returned to her body she was alive again, and her grateful people gave her to Hutu as his second wife.

Pare-ārau
A woman with loose morals

Pare-ārau is usually identified with the planet Jupiter, though sometimes with Saturn. It was recognised that this bright 'star' [whetū] moves in a different way from most others, and the explanation was that Pare-ārau is a promiscuous woman who goes wandering around at night, up to no good.

She was sometimes said to be the wife of Kōpū (Venus as the morning star), and some believed her to be the leader of the Milky Way, the star that precedes it.

Parikoritawa
A god in a tree

North of Parinui on the upper Whanganui River, on a high hill, Whirinaki, there stood a tawa tree named Parikoritawa. Long ago a woman named Matakaha went to get berries from Parikoritawa, but no sooner had she set to work than a man appeared from the tree. He was not an ordinary man, but half man and half atua. His name was Mata-o-te-rangi.

He made love to her, then gave her his instructions. If she had his daughter, the girl was to be named Parikoritawa after the tree. If she had a boy, he would be named Takaiteiwa, but in this case the child would emerge from her back between the shoulders, and she would die.

The child was a boy. He was born in the same way that the cicada emerges from its nymphal husk, and the mother died. An uncle cared for the boy, and he grew up to be the greatest tohunga in the upper Whanganui region.

Patito
A dead man who came back

This man died and went down to Te Rēinga, leaving a son, Toakai. Down below he heard much about this son's prowess as a warrior, so he decided upon a trial of strength – for in his time he had been an expert spearsman.

Patito sought out Toakai in the world and challenged him to a duel with spears. Although Toakai was the champion warrior of his Ngā Puhi people, he was unable to ward off his father's thrusts.

Satisfied with his victory, the old man went back down. If his son had proved the better spearsman, Patito would have continued to live upon the earth and humans would not have been subject to death.

Pawa
Captain of the *Horouta*

According to East Coast tradition, the *Horouta* sailed from Hawaiki with a precious cargo of kūmara and other treasures under the command of Pawa (or Paoa). Off Whakatāne the vessel was damaged and required a new bowpiece, so Pawa took a party of men into the interior to fell a tree and adze a bowpiece. Needing a river to float this to the coast, he recited a chant and urinated, creating four rivers in this way.

But Pawa and his companions found that the bowpiece was not needed, because the *Horouta* was already rebuilt and had sailed on without them. They abandoned the bowpiece, which became a mountain, and went on by land. On the way Pawa created many landmarks, and many places received their names from events that occurred.

Then Pawa heard about an enormous kiwi, a bird that cannot be killed by human beings. Between Waipiro Bay and Tokomaru Bay he set a trap for this bird, a very large version of a rat trap. Some say this kiwi was a pet of Rongokako, a giant who was Pawa's enemy; certainly Rongokako came across the trap and dealt it a blow. The rod flew up and is now Mount Arowhana, far inland. The place where the trap stood has become the mountain known as Tāwhiti [Rat trap].

Pawa continued on, and created more landmarks in Tūranga. Among them is the long white headland which is his dog, turned to a cliff. This is Te Kurī-a-Pawa [Pawa's dog]; its English name is Young Nicks Head.

Pekehaua
A taniwha at Rotorua

Te Awahou Stream, flowing down to Lake Rotorua's north-western shore, has as its source a large, deep spring known as Te Waro-uri [The dark pit]; its English name is Taniwha Springs.

This spring was the home of a taniwha, Pekehaua, who devoured human beings. After many parties of travellers had been lost, some warriors of Ngāti Tama, led by Pitaka, made ready to fight him. They constructed a very large basket, plaited stout ropes, then made their way upstream, reciting ritual chants. On the bank by the spring, Pitaka and some companions entered the basket; it was weighted with stones, then lowered into the depths. Meanwhile the men on the bank recited chants to destroy the taniwha's powers.

At first the spines on the taniwha's back were angrily erect, then they grew soft as the chants took effect. When the men reached the bottom they found the taniwha stretched out there. Pitaka quietly placed a noose around its body, then tugged on a rope.

The people above recognised the signal and hauled up the men in the basket, and Pekehaua as well. They were pulled ashore, and the now helpless creature was clubbed to death. Inside its body were the bones of women, children and men, and garments and weapons of every kind.

Peketahi
A taniwha in the Waikato

In the Waikato region, Peketahi is a rangatira of the taniwha people. One of the stories about him concerns a tohunga, Poraka, who was a medium for Peketahi; he made him offerings, and the taniwha communicated with him.

One day Poraka told his daughter, Parekawa, to cut his hair. Since his head was tapu, Parekawa's hands had to remain tapu for some days afterwards. But while she was still in this condition, visitors arrived at her home. No-one else was there to cook for them, so Parekawa, deeply shamed, cooked the food despite her tapu hands.

So then the taniwha punished her for breaking the tapu. She went crazy and ran away, and in the end she jumped into a stream and disappeared from sight.

Parekawa made her way through the water then the earth, and came at last to a place where Peketahi and other taniwha were living. She was offered a meal, but Peketahi would not let her eat. He told her that if she ate the food down below, she would have to stay there always.

Because her father was Peketahi's medium, he allowed her to return to the world. By now she looked like a taniwha, and she was instructed to keep out of sight until she had jumped on to the tūāhu. The first time she was discovered, but the second time she reached the tūāhu. After rituals were performed, she once more assumed her human appearance.

Peketua
Origin of the tuatara

Reptiles are generally held to be offspring of Punga, but in some east coast traditions the tuatara was created by Peketua. This man made an egg from clay and endowed it with life; it cracked open, and out came the tuatara.

Sometimes Peketua has a wife, Mihamiha, and these two are the parents of all reptiles and insects.

Pikiao
Ancestor of Ngāti Pikiao

This high-ranking rangatira lived at Ōwhata on the eastern shore of Lake Rotorua. He was sixth in descent from Tama-te-kapua, captain of *Te Arawa* on its voyage from Hawaiki.

When Pikiao's first wife Rakeiti gave him only daughters, Pikiao sought another wife. He travelled across the island to a Ngāti Maniapoto community on the slopes of Mount Pirongia and there married a woman named Rereiao. Her first child proved to be a boy and was named

Hekemaru. In due course he became an important ancestor in this region.

Later Pikiao returned to his first wife and she at last bore a son, Tamakari. This man's descendants became Ngāti Pikiao, who belong to Lake Rotoiti.

Pikopiko-i-whiti
A harbour at Hawaiki

In accounts of ancestral voyages from Hawaiki to Aotearoa, the waka sometimes sets sail from a harbour or river mouth named Pikopiko-i-whiti. In a sense this waterway makes possible the voyages of the vessels that are launched there.

There were other beliefs. A South Island authority, Tāre Tikao, considered the earth to be circular (like a plate) and 'the sands at Pikopiko-i-whiti' [te one i Pikopiko-i-whiti] to be a sandbank that stretched around the world as a rim, restraining the oceans. This encircling sandbank was itself held in place by Hine-ahu-one [Woman formed from sand].

Pokopoko
A taniwha at Kaipara

According to one account, Pokopoko was the great taniwha of the Kaipara Harbour. He would assemble his taniwha followers, watch them gambolling, then place his red-ochre mark upon their backs.

Nine generations ago a tohunga named Mawe at Taiāmai (inland from the Bay of Islands) harboured a grudge against the people of Ngāti Whātua, so came in secret and recited chants calling upon Pokopoko to rise and destroy the Ōkāka Pā. In response Pokopoko raised his voice like thunder, summoned the wind and waves, burrowed under the cliff and brought the hill and pā crashing into the water.

Other authorities say Pokopoko was a man, not a taniwha, and that he was given his full name, Pokopoko-herehere-taniwha [Pokopoko who binds taniwha], after he fought and conquered an army of taniwha. When this man died he was given sea-burial, as he had wished, at the entrance to the Kaipara Harbour. After this, when the harbour was rough the people would say, 'Pokopoko's wrath is kindled.' When the waters were calm they remarked, 'Pokopoko is happy.'

It seems that this man, like some others, was thought to have become a taniwha after his death.

Ponaturi
Uncanny beings in the ocean

These supernatural beings resemble people. They live in the sea and sometimes come ashore, especially at night; their footprints used to be seen on the beach in the morning. They are generally hostile to humans. The hero Tāwhaki, in one version of his story, avenges his father's death and his mother's enslavement at the hands of the Ponaturi.

Porourangi
Founding ancestor of Ngāti Porou

This high-ranking man was a descendant of Paikea, who rode a whale from Hawaiki. He was a very tapu man, having inherited the extreme tapu of his ancestor Pouheni (a son of Paikea).

Porourangi is an important ancestor of Ngāti Porou, a people who take their name from him, and he is as well an ancestor of peoples right down the east coast from Tūranga (the Gisborne district) to the Wairarapa.

After his death his widow Hāmō married one of his brothers, Tahu (or Tahu-pōtiki). Tahu's descendants moved south, and some became Ngāi Tahu in the South Island.

Pōtaka-tawhiti
A chief's pet

In the traditions of the Arawa peoples, a dog named Pōtaka-tawhiti belonged to the great rangatira Hou (or Hou-mai-tawhiti). Another leading man, Uenuku, was suffering from a boil, and Pōtaka-tawhiti ate the discarded dressings. Since this was a terrible insult, Uenuku and his son Toi at once killed and ate the animal. Hou's sons Tama-te-kapua and Whakatūria went searching for Pōtaka-tawhiti, calling as they went, and when they reached Toi's village the dog howled his reply from inside Toi's stomach.

This was the cause of a great war between Hou's people and those of Uenuku. The struggle ended with the migration to Aotearoa of Tama-te-kapua and his followers.

Another dog called Pōtaka-tawhiti belonged to the Arawa explorer Īhenga. While this early ancestor was hunting kiwi in the interior, his dog ran on ahead and came upon a lake full of little fish. Pōtaka-tawhiti gulped some down, ran back and promptly brought them up again. Seeing the whitebait wriggling on the ground, Ihenga knew his dog had discovered a lake that would be a treasure for his people.

Pou

Treasures from Hawaiki

The best known tradition about Pou, or Pou-rangahua, is that one day this man left his home at Tūranga (Gisborne) and travelled to Hawaiki; some say he was carried off by the taniwha Ruamano, others that his waka was blown there in a storm. After a while he became homesick and Tāne, the leading rangatira at Hawaiki, allowed him to fly home on a giant bird named Te Manu-nui-a-Ruakapanga [Ruakapanga's great bird]. As a farewell present, Tāne gave him two baskets of kūmara. Lastly he warned him to treat the bird well.

But as they approached Tūranga, Pou pulled a feather from under the bird's wing (it fell into the ocean and grew into the first kahikatea tree). And he made the bird take him all the way home, delaying the creature so much that on the return flight he was killed by the demonic Tama-i-waho.

At Whangaparāoa in the southern Bay of Plenty, the myth takes a different form. Pou brings two plumes from Ruakapanga's great bird but he travels by waka, not on the bird's back, and he is responsible as well for the arrival of an important fish, the moki. Every winter these tapu fish migrate from Hawaiki to Whangaparāoa and are caught by the people there.

Another tradition, also belonging to Te Whānau-a-Apanui, tells how Pou arranged for great schools of kahawai to migrate each summer to the mouth of the Mōtū River.

Poutini
The origin of greenstone

The usual explanation for the origin of greenstone is that Ngahue and his pet fish Poutini were chased from Hawaiki to Aotearoa by their enemy Hine-tua-hōanga, and that in this country the fish turned into greenstone.

In other traditions Poutini, while still greenstone, is a star (which has not been identified). It is explained that 'One of the chiefs living in the sky is the star Poutini . . . Poutini's people are greenstone. Those people migrated here from Hawaiki, having been attacked by enemies. They came down from the sky, but their principal rangatira, Poutini, remained there.'

Poutū-te-rangi
A harvest star

Poutū-te-rangi is usually identified with the star Altair. His reappearance in the east before sunrise during the ninth month of the Māori year (February-March) marked the approach of autumn, and the tenth month (March-April) was often known by his name.

Arriving at this time, Poutū-te-rangi was one of the main food-bringing stars. In some parts of the country he presides over the kūmara harvest itself. Elsewhere he tells the people to prepare for the harvest, and Whānui then brings it.

Puanga
The start of the new year

Puanga is the star Rigel in the constellation of Orion. While the rising of Matariki (the Pleiades) marked the start of the new year in many parts of the country, in the Far North and the South Island the new year began after Puanga had come up brilliantly at dawn in the east. This took place in mid-June (a month after the rising of the Pleiades). Often the start of the year was calculated from the first new moon following the rising of Puanga.

Puanga was often believed to be female and was regarded as one of the most beautiful of stars.

Pūhaorangi
A lover from the sky

The stories differ, but all agree that Pūhaorangi was a man in the sky who in ancient times came down to earth to visit a human woman, Kura-i-monoa (or Te Kura-nui-a-monoa), whose earthly husband was Toi. Some say he came as a pigeon, which Te Kura fondled, others that in the dark house she thought him her husband. She bore his son Oho-mai-rangi [Oho from the sky].

Puha-o-te-rangi
A high-ranking Whanganui man

This ancestor is said to have been so tapu that most people did not greet him by pressing their nose to his nose [hongi] in the usual way, but instead pressed their nose to his knee – for his head was too sacred to be in contact with common people. Among his descendants are people belonging to the Whanganui region and the coastal strip extending northwards to Taranaki, also some of Ngāti Tūwharetoa in the Taupō region.

Puhi
A journey northwards

This man was a younger brother of Tōroa, who captained the *Mātaatua* on its voyage from Hawaiki. At first Puhi lived with his relatives at Whakatāne, but after a quarrel with Tōroa he left to find a new home.

He and his people sailed north in *Mātaatua*. Some say they went right up the east coast, others that at Tāmaki they portaged the vessel across to the Manukau Harbour, continued north to Hokianga, lived there for a while, then dragged their ship across to Kerikeri. All agree that Puhi and his people made their home at Takou Bay (just north of the Bay of Islands) and that *Mātaatua*, turned to stone, lies at the mouth of a little river there, the Kopua-kawai.

Puhi is an important ancestor of Ngā Puhi, who are sometimes said to take their name from him. Some say his full name was Puhi-kai-ariki and that his grandson was the great rangatira Rāhiri.

Punga
Parent of ugly creatures

There had to be a reason for the presence of ugly nasty creatures, and that reason was Punga. Sometimes he is the father of reptiles, sharks, and fish such as stingrays. In one region he is the father of marine mammals.

While Punga is generally male, in one story the creator Tāne takes to wife a woman named Punga who becomes the mother of insects. It seems to have been thought that the ugliest of all insects was the giant wētā, because this was known as Punga's wētā.

Pururau
An extraordinary fish

This fish was a tipua, an uncanny being. He was a kahawai, and was first sighted near Whangaparāoa in the Bay of Plenty, where kahawai are plentiful. Apart from his enormous size, he could be recognised by the fact that his head was always partly above the water and had a small tree growing upon it.

A man and woman, Tāne-patua and Mamoe, decided to capture Pururau. For months they followed the fish in their waka, taking with them a kahawai net of great mana and tapu. After Pururau had swum around the east coast and across to the west coast, they caught him at last at Waingongoro in southern Taranaki.

Pū-tē-hue
Origin of the gourd

Gourds were carefully cultivated. In summer the young fruit were enjoyed as a vegetable, but the plant was grown mainly for the ripened fruit, which became containers used for many purposes.

Among Ngāti Awa in the Bay of Plenty, the origin of the gourd plant was Pū-tē-hue, a female who was the last-born of the children of Tāne and Hine-rauāmoa.

Rāhiri
A northern ancestor

Nearly all of Ngā Puhi in the Far North trace descent from Rāhiri, whose grandfather Puhi came from Hawaiki on the *Mātaatua*. Puhi travelled north from Whakatāne to Hokianga, married there and had a daughter; this girl's name is usually given as Ihenga-parāoa, though the traditions vary. She married Tauramoko, a descendant of Nuku-tawhiti. Rāhiri was their son.

Rāhiri was born about sixteen generations ago at the foot of Whiria Hill at Pakanae, on the southern shore of the Hokianga Harbour. He had three wives. His first wife, Āhua-iti of Ngāi Tāhuhu, lived near Kaikohe, and Rāhiri stayed with her there for a while, but they quarrelled when she offered her brothers a meal of fernroot that had been set aside for Rāhiri. So they separated, but she afterwards bore his son, Uenuku-kūare. This man had many famous descendants.

Rāhiri's second wife, Whakaruru, had a son named Kaharau; many peoples trace their descent to him. His third wife was Moetonga.

Rakahore
Father of rocks

Rakahore is the origin of rocks of all kinds. Along with Hine-one [Sand woman] and Hine-tuakirikiri [Gravel woman] he protects the sides of Papa, the earth, from the attacks of Hine-moana [Ocean woman].

Raka-maomao
Father of the south wind

Raka-maomao is associated especially with the cold south wind, which is often his youngest child. Other winds as well are sometimes his progeny.

Tāwhirimātea is also regarded as the parent of winds, and the existence of these two figures is variously explained. Sometimes strong winds are the offspring of Tāwhirimātea and ordinary winds the children of Raka-maomao.

Raka-taura
Tohunga of the *Tainui*

In traditions about voyages from Hawaiki to Aotearoa, each waka has a leading tohunga. In the story of the *Tainui* there is a struggle between the ship's captain, Hoturoa, and its main tohunga, Raka-taura.

Some say Raka-taura was a lazy man, others that he was a thief. Certainly Hoturoa did not want him; he took another tohunga, Riu-ki-uta, and thought he had left Raka behind. Some say that Raka turned into a rat and hid on board; others that he and his wife rode on the back of their people's taniwha, Pane-iraira, or that they walked, or swam, across the ocean. Finally Raka and Hoturoa were reconciled, and near Maketū at Kāwhia they established sacred landmarks.

With his wife, Kahu-keke (or Kahu-rere), Raka then travelled through the territory of the Tainui peoples, inspecting the land and establishing mauri, brought from Hawaiki, to keep the birds in the forested ranges.

Rākeiao
A warrior with special powers

Hordes of dragonflies under the command of Rākeiao drove from the Rotorua region the early Maruiwi people whom the ancestors of Te Arawa had found there on their arrival, and who at this time were still living amongst them.

A son of the great Rangitihi and his wife Manawa-kotokoto, Rākeiao spent his later years at Lake Ōkataina. His descendants continued to live there.

Rangi
The sky father

Rangi's name means Sky. The world came into being when Rangi and Papa, the first parents, were separated by their son Tāne. Rangi was thrust high above his wife Papa, the earth, so that there would be room for people to move around, and light could enter the world. He was accompanied only by his son Tāwhirimātea, the wind.

Rangi is the first male and Papa the first female, and at the same time

Rangi is the sky and Papa the earth. This means that human society and the physical world came into existence at the same time. Each is inseparable from the other.

Being the first male, Rangi in important respects set the pattern for his male descendants. Coming as he does at the very beginning, he is an unspecialised figure; later male ancestors establish patterns of behaviour in more specific ways. But men's general nature is due to Rangi. Like him, men (in general) are high, associated with light, and tapu. Women on the other hand are like their mother Papa. While their fertility and their skills are essential to the continuance of human life and they are greatly loved and valued, they are in general of lower status than men.

Rangi and Papa are so huge, always so close to humans, that they are generalised figures and often rather passive. Their main role is to be themselves, and so provide the conditions for human existence.

Rangiātea
A sacred place

Rangiātea [Clear sky] is generally regarded as a sacred place of origin in Hawaiki. It is best known from proverbial sayings, such as 'I cannot be lost, I am the seed scattered from Rangiātea' [E kore au e ngaro, te kākano i ruia mai i Rangiātea]. A people whose ancestors came from Rangiātea and successfully crossed the wide seas to Aotearoa cannot be defeated. They will forever survive and flourish.

It seems that in earlier times such sayings were especially important on the west coast of the North Island. In that region Rangiātea was usually believed to be a shrine, sacred house, or mountain in Hawaiki.

Another ancient tradition locates Rangiātea in the highest of the skies. There, on the Rauroha marae, this sacred building is the source of life and ritual power and also, for some persons of mana, the final destination of the wairua after death.

Māori settlers may have come to Aotearoa from the Society Islands, where the culture is broadly similar. One of the islands in this group, Ra'iatea, has a name that, allowing for a sound shift, is identical with that of Rangiātea. Ra'iatea is now often regarded as the place referred to in the saying about 'the seed scattered from Rangiātea'.

Rangiriri
The source of fish

In the sea near Hawaiki there is a spring which is the origin and home of the fish and other creatures in the ocean. Often this is known as the spring at Rangiriri [te puna i Rangiriri]. The name occurs in fishermen's chants that ask Tangaroa, father of the fish, to send his children from the spring at Rangiriri.

Rangitāne
A founding ancestor

The Rangitāne people trace their descent from Rangitāne, a grandson of Whātonga. This man Whātonga, they believe, was one of three rangatira who arrived from Hawaiki on the *Kurahaupō*, landing at Nukutaurua on Māhia Peninsula.

Rangitāne lived in Heretaunga (Hawke's Bay), and with his uncle Tara he took part in fighting in the region. He was also known as Tāne-nui-a-rangi and as Rangitāne-nui-a-rangi.

At one time the descendants of Rangitāne were (in alliance with the closely related Ngāi Tara) the dominant people in a vast area which included the region now known as Hawke's Bay, the Wellington district up to Dannevirke, the Marlborough Sounds, and part of Nelson. They are now based in the Manawatū region.

Rangitihi
An important Arawa ancestor

Rangitihi was a great-great-grandson of Tama-te-kapua, who had captained *Te Arawa* on its voyage from Hawaiki. He married three sisters, then later took a fourth wife. His eight children became the ancestors of most of the peoples in the Rotorua lakes district. They were Kawatapuārangi, Rākeiao, Apumoana, Rātōrua, Rangiwhakaekeau, Rangiaowhia, Tauruao (a daughter), and Tūhourangi.

Rarotonga
Firmly rooted

Rarotonga is mentioned in tradition as a place associated with Hawaiki. In proverbs it is a place where things are established firmly and cannot be shaken; one saying asserts that 'We cannot be overcome, we are a firmly rooted cabbage tree from Rarotonga' [E kore e riro, he tī tāmore nō Rarotonga].

This is an affirmation of strength. The persons to whom the saying is applied are as difficult to move as a cabbage tree, with its long taproot. And the cabbage tree, being so strongly rooted, belongs to Rarotonga.

Rata
Revenge for a father's death

Wahieroa, son of Tāwhaki, was killed by Matuku-tangotango, a demonic being. His own son, Rata, grew up knowing it was his sacred duty to avenge his father's death.

For this he needed a waka, so he felled a tall tōtara. At dawn next day he returned to adze his tree, but to his astonishment found it upright once more. Again he cut it down, but again next day the tree was standing there. Realising a trick was being played, he felled the tree then hid nearby.

Soon he heard the sound of chanting as the multitude of the Hākuturi approached his tree. Their chant was so powerful that the tree returned to its stump, the chips flew back, and soon it was growing there as it had done before.

The multitude of the Hākuturi discovered Rata and they upbraided him: 'It was your doing, for cutting down Tāne's tapu forest without authority. Didn't you think to go to your ancestors, so they could give their assent?'

Rata was shamed by their words, and ever since this time people have performed the proper rituals before cutting down a tōtara or any other important tree.

The Hākuturi themselves adzed Rata's waka, completing it with extraordinary speed. They then, it is sometimes said, formed his crew as he set out to accomplish his task. At dawn they launched their waka; Rata recited a ritual chant, and it sped across the sea to Matuku-tangotango's home. Then Rata killed the monster and avenged his father's death.

Rats
Weak, greedy, cunning

Having an abundance of fish but very little meat, Polynesians valued their mainly herbivorous rats [kiore] and carefully transported them from one island to another.

Rats run considerable distances at night from one feeding ground to another, scampering in single file along narrow paths that keep to the highest ground. Traps were laid along these paths and the tiny creatures were singed or plucked. They were then barbecued, or cooked in vessels and potted in their own fat ready to be presented to guests.

It was thought that rats could cross water, still in single file, each holding in its mouth the tail of the rat in front; in this formation they safely crossed rivers and even Raukawa (Cook Strait). Some said that in the beginning, rats had swum the wide ocean between Hawaiki and Aotearoa.

Rats were proverbially weak, but also greedy and cunning at finding stored food. People could be likened to them for this reason.

Raukata-ura
A powerful ancestor in the north

In the Far North, Raukata-ura [Crimson Raukata] introduced music to the world. Her flute was once the tough leathery cocoon of the case moth, but later she went to live in this cocoon. Since she has lost her flute, her music now takes the form of sudden, unintelligible noises heard in the forest.

When enemy sorcery had to be countered by the tohunga, Raukata-ura's powers were employed. An effigy of Raukata-ura was placed upon a little mat and the tohunga asked her to go down to the underworld and take with her the wairua of the persons against whom his sorcery was directed. To ensure she did so, he turned her face downwards.

When war was imminent, Raukata-ura was again involved. Sometimes the tohunga led his people into battle with an effigy of Rakata-ura in one hand and his spear in the other.

Raukata-uri and Raukata-mea
Originators of the arts of pleasure

Games, music and dancing were introduced to the world by Raukata-uri [Dark Raukata] and her sister Raukata-mea [Red Raukata]. Sometimes Raukata-uri occurs on her own in these stories. When the two are spoken of together, Raukata-uri is always mentioned first.

In the forest Raukata-uri is an elusive presence. The case moth is thought to be her flute, or the woman herself; the cicada with its insistent song is sometimes said to be her; the mountain foxglove found on Taranaki (Mount Egmont) is her gourd plant; and some say her daughter is Whēke, 'a voice heard in the forest, a female who sings to the world'.

In the story of Tinirau and Kae, Kae visits Tinirau on his island and is kindly treated, then returns home on the back of Tinirau's pet whale. But Kae kills and eats the whale, and Tinirau plans revenge. To this end he summons his sisters Raukata-uri and Raukata-mea, with others, and sends them in search of Kae. At each village they teach the people the arts of Raukata-uri, such as dancing and singing, dart-throwing, top-spinning and string games. Finally, when all else fails, an erotic dance makes Kae laugh, revealing crooked teeth that betray his identity. By magical means the women carry Kae back to Tinirau's island, and there he is killed.

Raukawa
Founder of Ngāti Raukawa

Raukawa was the son of Tūrongo and Māhina-ā-rangi, whose marriage joined the descent lines of the Waikato and East Coast peoples. When he in his turn married Tūrongo-ihi, a descendant of Tia, he allied his Waikato peoples with the peoples of Te Arawa.

Raukawa's son Rereahu had many children, who became famous. Among them were Maniapoto and Matakore, each the founding ancestor of a people, and a daughter, Te Rongorito, who was very influential.

Raukawa himself became the founding ancestor of Ngāti Raukawa, in the region around Mount Maungatautari (between the present towns of Te Awamutu and Putaruru). In the early 1820s, sections of these people migrated to Te Whanga-nui-a-Tara (the Wellington region).

Rauru
The first carver

Many different peoples claim Rauru as their early ancestor, and the traditions about him vary accordingly. On the East Coast he is frequently the son of Toi, the first person to live in this land; on the west coast of the North Island (where Toi is often said to have lived not in Aotearoa but in Hawaiki), he is generally Toi's grandson.

He is an important ancestor of the Tauranga peoples, to whom he is known as Rauru-kī-tahi. This name means literally 'Rauru who spoke only once'. The implication is that Rauru always kept his word, also that he commanded such unquestioning obedience that he never had to repeat an order.

In southern Taranaki the people of Ngā Rauru have taken his name, and regard him as an ancestor who lived in Hawaiki before the departure of the *Aotea*.

Rauru is regarded in many regions as the originator of the art of wood carving.

Rehua
A great rangatira in the sky

Rehua is a very tapu man who lives in the highest of the skies, often the tenth sky. According to Ngāi Tahu in the south, Rehua was the eldest son of Rangi the sky and Papa the earth; he first appeared as lightning, but assumed human form when he ascended to the skies.

His younger brother, Tāne, later went up to visit him, then was shocked when Rehua prepared a meal by untying his long hair and shaking into a vessel the birds that have been feeding on the lice on his head. When these birds – they were tūī – had been cooked by attendants and placed before them, Tāne would not touch them, because they had fed on the lice that had fed on Rehua's tapu head. Tāne, however, received permission to take the birds down to the earth, and was told how to snare them. As well he took the trees with the fruits on which the birds feed; and so we now have birds and forests.

Rehua is also a bright, powerful star. Among some peoples, such as Tūhoe, he was identified with Antares. To others he was Betelgeuse, or sometimes Sirius.

Living as he does in the highest of the skies, Rehua inhabits the realm where there is eternal life. He can therefore 'cure the blind, resuscitate the dead, and cure all diseases'.

Rei-tū and Rei-pae
Northern ancestors

The stories vary, but these women are usually considered to be daughters of Tuihu, a rangatira in the southern Waikato who was a great-grandson of Whatihua and Apakura. A young rangatira from the north, Ueoneone, visited their home and fell in love with Rei-tū. After returning to Whangapē he called his great bird and told it to fetch her.

The bird flew off, and landed by the porch of the house where Rei-tū and Rei-pae were living. When it conveyed its message, Rei-tū agreed to go. Then Rei-pae begged to be taken as well, so they both climbed on the huge back and flew north. Near the district now known as Whāngārei, Rei-pae asked to be let down to relieve herself. They landed near a village and she decided to stay there, while the bird flew on with Rei-tū.

Rei-pae married Tāhuhu-pōtiki, a rangatira in the village where she had been left, while Rei-tū married Ueoneone. Both women became important ancestors.

Reptiles
Enemies of human beings

Geckos and tuatara were believed to have extraordinary powers and were regarded with fear and awe. They were, it seems, thought to be anomalous creatures, closely related to fish yet living on the land and even, in some cases, climbing trees. Green geckos were especially dreaded when they lifted their heads and emitted chattering sounds thought to be laughter. This was a terrible omen.

Most illness was thought to be caused by a gecko's having invaded the person's body. Such a gecko might have been sent by an atua as a punishment for having broken a tapu restriction, perhaps unknowingly, or it might have come from a sorcerer. If all went well, a tohunga could expel the gecko and heal the patient.

Atua might manifest themselves as geckos, birds or spiders, and those that took the form of geckos were especially feared. Yet the powers of such spirits were sometimes employed for the benefit of human beings, as when a captured gecko was ceremonially released to watch over a burial cave or the mauri of a food resource.

Tuatara are ancient reptiles much larger than geckos, up to sixty centimetres in length, and the male has a row of spines on his head and back which he erects, when excited, in an alarming manner. Yet while they were feared, they were not dreaded as geckos were. They were even eaten.

Reptiles [ngārara] were generally regarded as the offspring of Punga, whose children are all ugly. At first they lived in the sea, then they became dissatisfied and moved to their present home.

Rona
The woman in the moon

In the Far North, Rona is a woman who set out with her gourd one night to draw water. When the moon went behind a cloud she stumbled among the bushes, and cursed the moon for not giving light. So then the enraged moon came down and seized her. Rona clung to a tree but it was pulled from the ground, roots and all. She was carried right up to the moon, along with the tree and her gourd, and she can be seen up there when the moon is full.

Rongo
Origin of the kūmara

The kūmara, or sweet potato, was the most highly valued of plants. In some regions its father Rongo is a son of Rangi and Papa, while elsewhere he is a son of Tāne and a grandson of these first parents.

There are the many extended versions of his name. Some belong to Rongo himself, who brings the kūmara into existence, while others refer to secondary figures who later convey the kūmara to human beings. In Ngāti Awa tradition, for instance, there are two men with related names and roles. Rongo is a son of Tāne and father of the kūmara, while Rongo-māui is the man who later acquires the kūmara from the star Whānui and brings it down to the earth.

The kūmara was associated with peace and was seen as being opposed to the fernroot, which was often associated with warfare. Naturally then, Rongo is a peacemaker. In fact the word rongo means 'peace'.

Rongokako
Giant strides

This man arrived from Hawaiki, some say on the *Tākitimu*. He was a giant and could stride enormous distances.

There was a struggle between Rongokako and Pawa, who had come (most people say) on the *Horouta*. The two men raced down the East Coast; Rongokako took tremendous steps and Pawa was unable to catch him. In some places Rongokako's feet sank into flat rocks, and his footprints have been pointed out by later generations.

Pawa set a trap, hoping to catch Rongokako (or, some say, a giant kiwi that accompanied him). But his adversary sprang the trap and it is now a mountain.

Rongomai
A powerful god

In many parts of the country Rongomai was an atua who provided guidance and protection in times of war. In the Taupō region, he was the main god.

Te Heuheu Tūkino, the leading rangatira of Ngāti Tūwharetoa, explained in about 1905 that Rongomai still appeared to him: 'I am a Christian, but nevertheless my own god has not vanished. [Rongomai] is our guardian atua, and our god of war. His ariā [form] is a star; in the olden days it was a shooting star. Rongomai still appears on certain occasions. He has accompanied me on my travels at night. I was once riding along the shore of Lake Taupō, when the tohu [sign] of Rongomai appeared to follow me in the sky as I went on my way. He is my protector.'

Rongo-tākāwhiu
A fierce adversary

This was a man with dreadful powers. The Tūhoe people regarded him as a tohunga, a sorcerer who could bring about the death of an approaching enemy force (and who in this respect provided a precedent for human tohunga).

On the west coast of the North Island, Rongo-tākāwhiu was much feared. A poet complaining of illness blames it upon Rongo-tākāw[h]iu's 'destroying adzes' that have attacked his body.

In one tradition, Rongo-tākāwhiu has a nurturing role. According to Ngāti Raukawa and some others, the hero Whakatau was not born in the usual way but came from his mother's girdle, which she had thrown into the sea. At the bottom of the ocean Rongo-tākāwhiu gave life to the girdle, then cared for the boy he had produced.

But Rongo-tākāwhiu was still acting in character. The boy he reared had one sacred task in life, to avenge a murdered relative. The ritual chants he learnt from Rongo-tākāwhiu helped him to achieve his purpose.

Rongowhakaata
An ancestor in Tūranga

The Rongowhakaata people trace their descent from this rangatira, who was a great warrior. In Tūranga-nui (the Gisborne district) he ruled large pā at Manutūkē and Waerenga-a-hika.

Rongo-whakaata was a son of Tū-mauri-rere and a great-great-grandson of Porourangi. He married three sisters, Tūrahiri, Uetupue and Moetai.

Ruaeo
The giant who introduced lice

Ruaeo had intended to sail on *Te Arawa* on its voyage from Hawaiki to Aotearoa, but the captain, Tama-te-kapua, tricked him into going ashore and the ship sailed without him. Tama-te-kapua did this because he wanted Ruaeo's wife, Whakaotirangi, for himself.

Ruaeo, however, mounted his own expedition, caught up with Tama-te-kapua at Maketū and challenged him to single combat. Both these men were giants; Tama-te-kapua was three metres tall, Ruaeo even taller. There are no men like them now.

After a fearful struggle, Ruaeo pulled a handful of lice from a bag around his neck and rubbed them into Tama-te-kapua's hair. He then said, 'I've defeated you! You can keep our woman as your compensation, because you've been defeated.'

But that brave warrior Tama-te-kapua didn't hear a word, because he was itching and stinging and scratching. That is how lice came to Aotearoa.

Rua-ki-pōuri
A house in the ocean

In the Whanganui region it was believed that after the separation of Rangi the sky and Papa the earth, their sons Tāne and Tangaroa lived in a house in the ocean called Rua-ki-pōuri [Pit in darkness]. This house was the place from which the fish, little and big, were distributed throughout the ocean.

In other regions this house, while still associated with origins, was envisaged differently. In some parts of Taranaki, Rua-ki-pōuri was one of the names of Miru's house in the underworld.

Ruamano
An ocean taniwha

There are many stories about a famous taniwha of this name. In the Far North, Ruamano took the form of a mako shark. Further south, one belief was that he was the offspring of Tūtara-kauika, another that he sprang from Te Pupū, a personified form of volcanic fire. On the East Coast, Ruamano is one of a pair of taniwha that guided *Tākitimu* on its voyage to Aotearoa.

When a waka was overturned in a storm and the crew flung into the ocean, they might call upon Ruamano and sometimes he would take them to land. And in times of illness his assistance might be requested. A chant was recited and the affected part of the patient was sprinkled with salt water (which being associated with Ruamano, possessed his powers).

Ruapūtahanga
A famous Taranaki ancestor

This beautiful woman lived at Pātea in southern Taranaki; her people were Ngāti Ruanui. When a Waikato rangatira, Tūrongo, visited her home, she loved him and agreed to marry him.

So Tūrongo returned to Kāwhia to prepare for her arrival. He began enlarging his house, but his jealous half-brother Whatihua persuaded him that a smaller house would be better. Meanwhile Whatihua was secretly constructing a fine big house and laying in large supplies of food. When Ruapūtahanga arrived with a train of attendants, Tūrongo could not accommodate or feed them. Whatihua invited the party to stay in his new house, where he fed them well, and presently Ruapūtahanga changed her mind and married Whatihua instead.

But later, after she had borne two sons, Whatihua made a careless remark that insulted her. Deeply shamed, she set off on the long journey back to her home in southern Taranaki. She took the route along the shore, past precipitous cliffs, and at first she carried her baby son. But near Kāwhia she left him on the beach, knowing Whatihua would find him. And soon Whatihua came running up. He found the boy and put him on his back, then he saw Ruapūtahanga and implored her to return. But the woman kept on going, and crossed the Marokopa River. At Kaitangata Point she passed through a dangerous cavern, then the tide came in and it was too late for Whatihua to follow.

Ruapūtahanga did not return to Pātea. Instead she married a rangatira of Te Āti Awa whom she met in northern Taranaki. She had more sons, and when she eventually died and the news reached Kāwhia, her two sons there visited their half-brothers in Taranaki to mourn her death.

Ruarangi and Tawhaitū
The wife stolen by a fairy

One day when Ruarangi was away, a fairy [patupaiarehe] man visited their home, seized his wife Tawhaitū and carried her off. On Ruarangi's return his son told what had happened and the two of them wept together.

That night the wairua of another son, who had died, visited their house and told Ruarangi what to do: 'Don't cry any more. You must set out, and keep going until you reach the third river. You must stop and light a fire, catch a pig, and throw it on the fire.'

Ruarangi did this, and the smoke bearing the smell of pork drifted through the forest. It reached Tawhaitū and she wept, saying to herself, 'Perhaps this smoke is from Ruarangi.'

She followed it and came to Ruarangi. They returned home, but the fairy returned that night and carried her off once more.

Again Ruarangi and his son wept together, and again the dead son came to them: 'Don't cry any more. You must go again, and take with you a cooking pot and a gourd. When you have reached the third river, light another fire. Kill another pig and cook it in the pot, then dig for red ochre. Cook the pig's fat with the red ochre, fill the gourd with the mixture and bring it back home with you.'

Ruarangi returned to the forest, and the smoke from his fire once more reached Tawhaitū. Again she found him, and together they dug the red ochre. They carried it home and painted their house and marae, leaving the ridgepole of the house unpainted as an escape route for the fairy.

When he came he stayed a short distance away, afraid of the red ochre. He climbed to the ridgepole, but could still find no way of entering the house. He sang a lament acknowledging that the fairy people cannot live with human beings but must remain apart, then he rose up to his mountain home.

Ruatāne and Tarapikau
Rival fairy rangatira

Ruatāne was the rangatira of the fairies [patupaiarehe] in the region extending from Te Aroha through to the Moehau Range. Far to the south, on Mount Maungatautari and the Rangitoto Range north of Lake Taupō, the fairy rangatira was Tarapikau.

One day a human woman was gathering tawa berries in forests near the Rangitoto Range, in the territory of Tarapikau, when she was kidnapped by Ruatāne and carried off to Te Aroha. The wairua of her relatives found her there, and sent a messenger asking for Tarapikau's assistance.

Tarapikau told the messenger to go that night and encourage the Te Aroha fairies to dance haka; the messenger did so, and just before dawn the exhausted fairies fell fast asleep. Then Tarapikau and his men made a hole in the thatch of the house, found the woman and carried her off.

Soon they returned her to her people.

When Ruatāne found the woman gone, he knew Tarapikau had taken her and he set out with an army. But when he saw Tarapikau's warriors at Paewhenua, in the Rangitoto foothills, he realised they were too numerous for his forces to engage and he went back home.

Tarapikau's warriors are still at Paewhenua. They take the form of limestone rocks on a hillside there.

Ruatapu
An insult avenged

In Hawaiki, one of the sons of the great Uenuku was of unequal parentage. On his father's side he was of high rank, but his mother was little better than a slave.

After Ruatapu had become a man, he and his brothers adzed a waka. When all was done and the young men were adorning themselves for the first, ceremonial voyage, Uenuku anointed and combed the heads of his seven-score sons – all except Ruatapu. Uenuku told Ruatapu that he could not anoint his head because he was only a bastard, of no importance.

Ruatapu wept with shame and planned his revenge. He bored a hole in the bilge of the vessel, then put to sea with his brothers, his foot over the hole. When the land was lost to sight, he let the water come in. The waka overturned and Ruatapu drowned his brothers one by one.

But Paikea could not be drowned, for he was borne up by ritual chants. Accepting this, Ruatapu offered advice. He foretold that after Paikea had reached the land, he, Ruatapu, would arrive in the early summer in the form of immense waves, and he cautioned that the people must gather on the high ground to survive the flood.

Paikea rode a whale to Aotearoa, and Ruatapu arrived in the early summer as he had said he would.

This is the myth as it is known to the people of Ngāti Porou, on the East Coast north of Gisborne. The story explains the origin of the high waves that do in this part of the country break on the shore in early summer, and at the same time it intensifies the reality, turning the waves into a flood. Further south, the story changed somewhat. In Heretaunga (Hawke's Bay), where these large waves of early summer do not occur, the waves in the myth break in winter, no doubt because of the rough weather experienced then.

Rua-taranaki
The first person to climb Taranaki

Mount Taranaki (Mount Egmont) is said by some to have received its present name after being climbed by Rua-taranaki, the first person to reach those snowy heights. This man Rua-taranaki belonged to an early people known as Te Kāhui Maunga [The assembly of mountains].

Others say it was Tahurangi who first climbed the mountain, and so laid claim to it.

Rua-te-pupuke
The origin of carving

In Ngāti Porou tradition, Rua-te-pupuke was the first person to gain a knowledge of carving. He acquired it from Tangaroa, who had kidnapped his son Te Manu-hau-turuki.

Te Manu had been sailing a toy boat on the beach when he was carried off by Tangaroa, taken down to his house in the sea and placed on the roof as a gable figure, a tekoteko. Rua-te-pupuke searched for him and finally found him there. An old woman advised Rua-te-pupuke that to overcome Tangaroa and his children he must block up the cracks in the house so that daylight could not enter.

In the evening Tangaroa appeared with his children (who were fish); they sang and danced, then slept. Next day these creatures of darkness did not know the sun had risen, and when Rua-te-pupuke pulled open the door they were caught in the light.

Rua-te-pupuke fought and killed them, avenging his son, then he burnt the house and brought back up the carved posts from its house. These became models for carvers in this world.

The victory over Tangaroa and his children was the occasion on which many of the different kinds of fish assumed their present forms, and dispersed to the places where they are now to be found.

Rua-te-pupuke is the best known of many personifications that represent forms of knowledge, the desire for knowledge, and its acquisition.

Rūaumoko
Origin of earthquakes

A son of Rangi and Papa, sky and earth, Rūaumoko was still in the womb when his parents were separated, so he remains there now. Sometimes he moves around inside his mother, causing earthquakes. By shaking her and turning her over, he divides the warmth of summer from the cold of winter.

Rūaumoko is sometimes held responsible for volcanic activity. And living as he does in the earth, he is often associated with death. In some accounts he is married to Hine-nui-te-pō, who presides over the underworld.

Rukutia
An originator of weaving

In a South Island myth, Rukutia leaves her ugly husband, Tama-nui-a-Raki, for the good-looking Tū-te-koropaka (or Tū-te-koropanga). Tama visits the underworld and his ancestors tattoo him, making him handsome, then he returns to the world and sets out in pursuit of his wife. He gets her back, kills her, then mourns her death. When the spring comes, she returns to life.

Elsewhere in Māori tradition, though not in this story, Rukutia is an originator of weaving and plaiting.

Ruru-teina
A youngest son

In a tale from the far south, Ruru-teina [Ruru junior] is the youngest son and is treated badly by his brothers. One day the brothers hear about a beautiful woman, Te Roronga-rahia, who lives some distance away. They set out to visit her home, and Ruru goes as their servant.

On their arrival, Ruru stays behind to look after the waka while the others are entertained in the village. Each brother keeps company with a woman there, and each of these women pretends to be Te Roronga-rahia.

Meanwhile Ruru comes across the real Te Roronga-rahia sitting quietly in her house with her servant. Every evening he visits her, and she falls in love with him.

Some days later the elder brothers prepare to return home. That night, Ruru hides Te Roronga-rahia and her servant inside the deck-house. Each of the brothers arrives with his woman, and they sail off.

The wind is against them, and they land in a strange country. Ruru is told to ask for fire at a settlement in the distance, and there he finds a giant reptile, an evil female named Te Ngārara-hua-rau (or Te Kārara-hua-rau) who tries to detain him.

Ruru escapes, and he and his brothers build a trap, a house with a carved figure of Ruru inside it. Presently Te Ngārara-hua-rau comes looking for Ruru; she enters the house and wraps her disgusting tail around the figure, thinking it Ruru himself. The brothers set fire to the house and the monster is burnt to death.

Then a fair wind sends them home to their parents. Each of the elder brothers claims that his wife is Te Roronga-rahia, but it is revealed that Ruru-teina himself is married to Te Roronga-rahia.

Sky
The eternal heights

The sky is the first father, Rangi (whose name means Sky). It is an immortal realm because of its height and inaccessibility, and because the lights that move around it live forever. The Sun, Moon and stars do not die like people on the earth.

In making human existence possible, these lights give life to human beings. Days and nights are created by the Sun, the year is created by the Sun's annual movements and the Moon's cycles, and the most important of the stars bring with them the seasons and their associated food resources.

In many places it was believed that a number of skies lie one above the other and that the highest is the most tapu and powerful of all. Some authorities speak of two skies, others of ten, eleven or twelve.

In several myths a man goes up to the skies to obtain a possession, or knowledge, from a person up there. The best known of these journeys are made by Tāne and Tāwhaki.

Stars
People in the sky

Tohunga with a special knowledge of the stars spent much time studying them. Since these shining persons follow in their movements and conjunctions a yearly cycle, as does the earth below, their rising and setting inevitably marked the progression of the seasons. As well, certain stars were believed to bring the seasons into existence and to send seasonal foods down to the earth.

Because the general movement of the stars is from east to west, a star or constellation that has been absent from the sky for a while will become visible again in the east just before dawn. The stars therefore, like the sun, were seen as coming from the direction of Hawaiki (which lies in the east). Since this mythical land was the main source of life and fertility, the association with Hawaiki supported the idea that some stars bring seasonal foods.

The stars were placed in the sky by Tāne. After he had pushed up his father Rangi the sky, people could move about on the earth but they were still in darkness. So to create light and make his father beautiful, Tāne flung up the stars, then the moon and the sun.

It was thought in some regions that when a person of consequence died, the left eye became a star.

Sun
The light of day

Daylight was associated with life and wellbeing, and darkness with weakness and sometimes death. As an extension of this idea, the rising sun and the east were associated with life, and the setting sun and the west with death. The rising sun was often greeted with a joyful song, while the evening was a time when people sang laments.

Because of this, east was a propitious direction. At divination ceremonies it was a good omen if rods fell towards the east, a bad one if they fell towards the west. Males were associated with the rising sun, females with the setting sun. The homeland of Hawaiki, the source of life, was generally believed to lie in the direction of the rising sun.

The Sun [Te Rā] was placed in the sky by Tāne after he had separated Rangi the sky and Papa the earth. Some peoples on the east coast believed that Tāne obtained the Sun, along with the Moon, from his younger brother, Tangotango.

Taha-rākau
A prudent, quick-witted man

Taha-rākau, a rangatira living at Tūranga (the Gisborne district), once set off with a single companion to visit Tapuae, whose home was at Te Rēinga in the Wairoa district. Taha-rākau's friend, Te Angiangi, wore his best clothes for the journey, but Taha-rākau wrapped up his good clothes and took two rain capes with him. And sure enough, in the end it rained. Te Angiangi's fine garments were soaked through, but Taha-rākau put on his rain capes and was quite comfortable.

At Te Rēinga he changed into his good clothes. And while they were being welcomed, he noticed that Tapuae's carved house was not inside a pā in the usual way but stood in the fields where enemies could reach it.

Later, when the visitors were being feasted, Tapuae asked Taha-rākau three questions, hoping to outwit him and diminish his mana. The first question was, 'Taha, wouldn't it have been better if a large party had escorted you?'

Taha-rākau calmly replied, 'When I've got my rain capes to protect me, that's a large enough party.'

The next question was, 'What do people live on in Tūranga?'

Taha-rākau told him, 'We eat from cabbage-tree ovens by day, and make love to our women at night.'

Again Tapuae felt that Taha-rākau had got the better of him. So he asked his last question: 'Taha-rākau, what is the mark of an aristocrat?'

And Taha-rākau, remembering how Tapuae's house was positioned, replied, 'A carved house standing inside a pā is the mark of an aristocrat. A carved house standing in the open, amongst cultivations, is food for fire.'

Once more Taha-rākau had outwitted his opponent. His sayings are still repeated today.

Tahu
Source of good things

Tahu represents food and plenty, tranquillity, and feasts. On the west coast of the North Island he is sometimes a son of Rangi the sky and Papa the earth.

One writer tells us Tahu is 'the source of good things, life and well-being, and joyful hearts. It is because of him that husbands love and care for their wives and children, and wives love and care for their children and husbands.'

He is often contrasted with Tū, who personifies warfare.

Tahu-pōtiki
Founder of Ngāi Tahu

This early ancestor lived on the East Coast of the North Island and was a brother of Porourangi, from whom the people of Ngāti Porou take their name. After Porourangi's death, Tahu-pōtiki married his widow Hāmō – it being customary for a surviving brother to marry the widow. Hāmō, who had borne Porourangi four children, had three more children in this marriage.

Tahu's descendants lived for a while in Tūranga (the Gisborne district), then made their way further south. Some lived for a time at Te Whanga-nui-a-Tara (the Wellington district). Eventually, perhaps late in the seventeenth century, some migrated to the South Island. There they fought with Ngāti Māmoe and Waitaha, the main peoples in possession of the island, and formed alliances with them through marriage. In time they won a leading position and were able to call the island Tahu's house [Te Whare o Tahu].

Tahurangi
The man who claimed Taranaki

Tahurangi is often said to have been the first man to climb Taranaki (Mount Egmont). He belonged to the Taranaki people who live near the mountain, and he climbed it to claim it for them. At the top he lit a fire so that all could see what he had done.

When misty clouds like smoke cling to the summit of Taranaki, these are from Tahurangi's fire.

Taiāmai
A bird from Hawaiki

A district often takes its name from one particular place, frequently a rock, where a significant event occurred. This place is the tino, the essence, of the entire region. Formerly such places were tapu and treated with great respect.

The district inland from the Bay of Islands is traditionally known as Taiāmai. Near the present town of Ōhaeawai, some 600 metres behind the post office, there stands a great block of lava more than three metres high. This is the tino of Taiāmai.

In the early days a white pigeon [kererū] appeared and drank from a pool in the rock. Seeing this strange beautiful bird, the rangatira of the local people told them, 'This bird is from Hawaiki; he is Taiāmai. He is tapu and will bring us great mana.'

Every afternoon Taiāmai came to drink from the rock. Then one evening a neighbouring rangatira, jealous of this mana, tried to capture the bird. It vanished into the rock, which from this time became known as Taiāmai.

Down through the generations, people passing tapu the rock would acknowledge its mana by observing the ceremony of uruuru-whenua. Plucking a twig, they would recite a ritual chant and lay the twig as an offering beside it.

Taiau
A fishing rock

The early ancestor Māia is best known for having brought the seeds of the gourd from Hawaiki to the Tūranga (Gisborne) district. As well, he created a valuable fishing rock. Standing one day by the Tūranganui River, Māia called to a girl, Taiau, on the opposite bank and told her to bring his waka to him. When she did so, he drowned her. But this was no arbitrary act of violence, because Taiau was transformed into a treasured fishing rock, Te Toka a Taiau [Taiau's rock].

This huge rock used to mark the boundary between the territory of Ngāti Porou to the north, and the lands belonging to the peoples of Tūranga. Now that the rock has been dynamited, a bridge serves this purpose.

Taikehu
An ancestor's fishing resources

In both Arawa and Tainui traditions, harbours that are rich fishing grounds are associated with an ancestor named Taikehu.

The Arawa peoples say that Taikehu arrived from Hawaiki on *Te Arawa* and began collecting sea food from a sandbank in the Tauranga Harbour near Katikati, which is known therefore as Te Ranga-a-Taikehu [Taikehu's sandbank].

The Tainui peoples believe that Taikehu came on their waka and settled at Tāmaki; in the Waitematā the *Tainui* was stranded for a while on a sandbank now known as Te Ranga-a-Taikehu [Taikehu's sandbank]. Afterwards Taikehu led an expedition to Manuka (the Manukau Harbour), where his party found an abundance of seafood. To take possession of these fishing grounds, Taikehu named the mullet leaping in the harbour 'the fearless children of Taikehu' [ngā tamariki toa o Taikehu].

Tainui
Waka of the Tainui peoples

When the *Tainui* was ready to set sail from Hawaiki to Aotearoa, the captain, Hoturoa, arranged for kūmara and other plants to be stowed on board.

Ngātoro-i-rangi had been chosen as tohunga, but he was kidnapped by Tama-te-kapua, captain of *Te Arawa*. Some say Raka-taura took his place, others that Raka had been deliberately left behind in Hawaiki, but crossed the ocean by methods of his own. Riu-ki-uta is generally thought to have replaced him as tohunga.

When *Tainui* made land on the East Coast at Whangaparāoa [Bay of whales] the crew had their famous encounter with the crew of *Te Arawa*, who had arrived just before them. The men of *Te Arawa* had erected their tūāhu, had tied a rope to a whale stranded on the beach, and were now exploring the hinterland. The crew of the *Tainui* deceived them by constructing their own tūāhu from materials they had dried by a fire, and by tying a dried rope of their own to the whale. Afterwards they argued successfully that their materials were older than those of the Arawa men and that this proved their prior claim to the land.

The *Tainui* then coasted north, leaving names and landmarks in the places the crew visited. Accounts differ as to the direction taken after the ship entered Tikapa-moana (the Hauraki Gulf). It is generally believed, though, that *Tainui* reached the west coast by being portaged across the Tāmaki Isthmus.

At first this could not be done. When the ship had been taken up the Tāmaki River and was to be dragged over to Manuka (the Manukau Harbour), it would not move forward on the skids. The reason was detected by Raka-taura; he discovered that Hoturoa's secondary wife, Marama, had broken tapu by having an affair with a slave. Marama sang a song admitting her guilt, the slave was sacrificed to the gods, other necessary rituals were performed, the men again pulled on the ropes, and the ship glided forward. Soon it drank the waters of Manuka.

Some of the crew, among them Riu-ki-uta, remained at Tāmaki; the others sailed south towards Kāwhia. On the way further landmarks were established and names were given to places they passed.

Some say the reconciliation between Hoturoa and Raka-taura occurred at Tāmaki, others that it took place at Kāwhia. Beside the harbour there, at Maketū, two tapu stone pillars, Hani and Puna, mark the positions of the prow and sternpost of *Tainui*. The ship itself lies buried, turned to stone, between them.

Nearby on a low hill a tūāhu and a house of learning [whare wānanga] were established. Hoturoa gave his daughter Kahu-keke to Raka as his wife, and Raka, with Kahu and other companions, set out on a long journey to place in the hills the mauri he had brought from Hawaiki.

Meanwhile Whakaotirangi, Hoturoa's principal wife, planted her kūmara. During the voyage the rest of the crew had eaten the seed kūmara they carried, but Whakaotirangi had prudently kept hers tied up in a corner of her basket. Now they were planted in soil brought from Hawaiki and they bore a heavy crop.

Taipō
Supernatural intruders

The word taipō refers to many kinds of unwanted supernatural visitors. It entered the language, it seems, in the middle of the nineteenth century, and is of unknown origin.

Takarangi and Rau-mahora
A marriage that brought peace

Takarangi was a great warrior of Ngāti Awa (who are known now as Te Āti Awa). In about 1750 he led an army against the Whakarewa Pā, in the territory of the Taranaki people.

He and his men besieged the pā, and its inhabitants suffered from hunger and thirst. Finally their rangatira, an old man named Rangi-rā-runga, mounted the palisades and asked his enemies for water. Some wanted to help, but others would not agree. Then Rangi-rā-runga caught sight of Takarangi and recognised him as their leader. In the proud language of warriors on the battlefield, he asked for Takarangi's assistance.

Takarangi consented to this, for though he had been eager for battle he had heard of the beauty of Rangi-rā-runga's daughter, Rau-mahora, and he felt pity for her and her people. He filled a gourd at a spring and carried it to the old man, and none of his people dared intervene. Rangi-rā-runga and his daughter drank, while the young man and the girl gazed at each other.

Rangi-rā-runga asked his daughter if she would marry Takarangi, and she agreed. The marriage brought a lasting peace.

Takere-piripiri
A guardian insulted

This reptile looked like a giant tuatara. He was the guardian of the Ōtautahanga Pā, a stronghold of Ngāti Raukawa, and every day received a basket of the best food. One day the rangatira's two grandchildren, a boy and a girl, were told to take Takere-piripiri his meal, but the smell of the steamed eels was too much for them and they ate until only the heads were left. So they put fern in the bottom of the basket, arranged the heads on top, and offered the basket to Takere-piripiri.

Finding the heads, the hungry reptile pursued the children and killed and ate them. But his anger was not assuaged. That night he abandoned his home and made his way north to the Maungakawa Range. There he found another home, in a cave near a track used by travellers crossing the mountains.

The people in the pā mourned the childrens' deaths but were greatly disturbed at the loss of their guardian. And in fact the pā was soon afterwards attacked and taken by enemies.

Takere-piripiri also came to grief. Since there was no-one to bring him offerings, he ate passing travellers. Most belonged to Ngāti Hauā, and in the end the warriors of these people succeeded in killing him..

Tākitimu
An ancestral waka

Peoples in certain parts of the East Coast, the South Island and the Far North trace their descent to ancestors who came from Hawaiki on the *Tākitimu*. Differing versions of the story are known in different parts of the country, and some accounts have been elaborated to include visits to all of these regions.

In the East Coast story there is often a preliminary episode in which two men, Ruawhārō and Tūpai, insult the great rangatira Uenuku and are treated roughly by him, then go to their grandfather, Timu-whakairia, for the ritual chants that will enable them to take their revenge. Afterwards they find Uenuku's people hauling their waka, the *Tākitimu*. Ruawhārō and Tūpai cut the ropes and then, reciting the appropriate chants, place before the ship four skids that prevent it from moving forward. When the vessel's owners cannot move it, the two men offer to do so; Ruawhārō chants the hauling song, while Tūpai puts in place another skid with special powers. The waka slides easily forward, and now belongs to Ruawhārō and Tūpai. In this way they revenge themselves for their injury.

They then prepare the *Tākitimu* for its voyage. As crew they take the previous owners, seven score men of high rank. As atua they put on board Kahukura, Tama-i-waho and others; these gods obey them because of their ritual chants. They take as well their five skids, their tapu knowledge, and the mauri of the whales which they have brought from Timu-whakairia's house.

Some say the leading men on the *Tākitimu*, apart from Ruawhārō and Tūpai, were Rongokako, Tamatea, and Tamatea's son Kahungunu. Others name Kiwa as the captain. Some believe that the famous Tamatea was born in Aotearoa, and most agree that Kahungunu was born here. Some claim that the giant Rongokako came by means of his own.

Because the gods, the knowledge, and the rangatira that arrived on the *Tākitimu* were highly tapu, the vessel itself was so tapu that food supplies could not be taken on board. By the time the crew reached the middle of the ocean they were suffering from hunger, so a man called down to the pāua, and multitudes of them rose up as food. This happened on several occasions, each time with shellfish of a different kind. Since the vessel was too tapu to contain cooked food, the people ate the shellfish raw – and that is why they are still often eaten raw.

The ship made landfall at Nukutaurua, at Te Māhia [the Māhia Peninsula]; some say it is still there now, along with its skids. Because the mauri of the whales was left there, and sand from Hawaiki, whales now beach themselves at Te Māhia.

Later, Ruawhārō travelled south along the coast of Heretaunga (Hawke's Bay), leaving his sons Matiu, Makaro and Moko-tuararo in places there. They turned to stone and became powerful mauri that attracted whales and other fish to those regions.

When the people of Ngāi Tahu migrated from the East Coast to the South Island, they brought the story of the *Tākitimu* with them. They now believed that *Tākitimu*, having sailed down the east coast of the North Island, continued on to the east coast of the South Island then was swamped by three waves. The vessel overturned and became the Tākitimu Mountains, the waves became high hills, and the captain, Tamatea, walked back along the coast creating landmarks as he went.

In the Far North it is said that *Tākitimu* made its way up there, and that the hull now lies by Tokerau (Doubtless Bay), turned to stone. Some people in the region trace descent from Tamatea.

Takurua
The winter star

Takurua is a name often given to Sirius, the brightest star in the sky. The Tūhoe people, probably others as well, say she is a woman who brings the winter. On cold nights she shines brightly to warn that there will be a hard frost.

Winter itself is often known as takurua. It is referred to poetically as Hine-takurua [Winter-woman].

There are those, however, who identify Sirius with Rehua.

Tama
The greenstone wives

Greenstone, or jade, was obtainable only in a few remote valleys in the South Island. The most famous was the Arahura Valley in Westland, and its presence there was explained by a tradition telling how Tama arrived from Hawaiki on the *Tairea* in search of his three runaway wives. At Arahura he found his wives, but his slave broke a tapu restriction and the atua punished Tama by turning the women into the different kinds of greenstone now to be found there.

Further south, in the fiords of Piopio-tahi (Milford Sound), a translucent kind of greenstone known as tangiwai is another of Tama's wives.

Tama-āhua
A flying man

In the early days at Waitōtara, in the Whanganui region, Tama-āhua used to project himself through the air without the use of wings. Some say he could do this because of his great mana, and that he lost his powers when he married.

Others maintain that Tama-āhua owed his power of flight to the possession of a feather called Te Rau-ā-moa [The moa feather], which had been plucked from under the wing of a giant bird. They speak of Tama-āhua's mana but do not say that he lost his powers.

Tama-i-rēia
Fairy battles

The fairy [tūrehu] people live on the hilltops and move around in mist and darkness. Two fairy peoples once lived in the Tāmaki (Auckland) region, one in the Waitakere Ranges and the other in the Hunua Ranges. A war began when Hine-mairangi, a high-born Hunua woman, eloped with Tama-i-rēia, leader of the Waitakere people.

The two forces met one night at Pakuranga, and at first neither side could gain the advantage. Then the Hunua tohunga made the sun rise before the proper time, and many of the Waitakere warriors died in the light.

The following night the Hunua people again advanced, but the Waitakere tohunga were ready for them. They made volcanoes erupt from the earth, and the Hunua warriors were driven back. When a change of wind brought the volcanic fires back towards the Waitakere forests, the tohunga sent rain to quench the flames.

The remains of the volcanoes are still at Tāmaki, and in the Waitakere Ranges there is still a much heavier rainfall than elsewhere in the region.

Tama-i-waho
A god in the sky

This powerful atua in the sky was a war god of a number of Bay of Plenty and East Coast peoples. His visible form was a star, which has not been identified. Before a battle he would be asked to foretell the outcome, and would reply by taking possession of a tohunga and speaking through him. He also warned of approaching enemies.

Tama-i-waho's position in the highest of the skies is associated with great power, including a knowledge of ritual chants. When visited by a stranger he may be helpful, but is more likely to destroy the intruder. A number of stories tell how the hero Tāwhaki climbed to the sky to visit him; some say Tāwhaki was killed, others that he obtained the knowledge he sought.

Tama-nui-a-Raki
The man who was tattooed

Because Tama-nui-a-Raki had an ugly face, Tū-te-koropaka was able to steal his wife. Learning for the first time that he was ugly, Tama made his way to the underworld and found two ancestors, Toka and Hā, who were tattooers. They were at first reluctant to tattoo him, saying the pain was bad as death, but Tama insisted. After many days it was done; he was carried to a house and began to recover. When his wounds healed he found that he was handsome.

Soon afterwards Tama set out to find his wife, Rukutia. He overcame the obstructing plants and other obstacles that her new husband, Tū-te-koropaka, had left in his path, and he approached their house. He entered, disguised as a slave, then eventually revealed himself to Rukutia. Seeing how handsome he now was, she begged to be taken back. But Tama had not forgiven his wife. He killed her, returned home with her body, buried her in a box, then sat mourning until the spring.

When the spring came, a humming blowfly told Tama that Rukutia had come back to life. He opened the box in which her body lay and he saw she was alive once more, and smiling at him.

Tama-o-hoi
A powerful atua

Tama-o-hoi is so old that some trace his descent to Māui, who fished up the land. His descendants include both humans and fairies. Some believe that his home is in Ruawāhia, the enormous crater in Mount Tarawera. When Ngātoro-i-rangi had arrived from Hawaiki and was exploring the countryside he was confronted by Tama-o-hoi, who resented this intrusion. Ngātoro-i-rangi stamped upon Mount Tarawera, forming Ruawāhia, and thrust Tama-o-hoi down inside. There he remained until 1886, when he burst free and caused a terrible volcanic eruption.

Tama-rereti
The waka in the sky

Tama-rereti possesses a ship, with sternpost, rope and anchor, which can be seen in the sky at night. Sometimes he has a fish hook rather than an anchor, and spends the night fishing. At dawn the vessel reaches land.

Usually his waka is identified with the Tail of the Scorpion in the constellation of Scorpius. Some say it is the *Uruao*; though others assign this name to a waka that brought the ancestors of the Waitaha people to Te Wai Pounamu (The South Island).

Tamatea
A great explorer

Tamatea is usually said to have captained the *Tākitimu* on its voyage from Hawaiki, though some say he was born in Aotearoa. All agree that he undertook ambitious journeys of exploration.

A number of extended names, such as Tamatea-ariki-nui [Tamatea the great lord], Tamatea-mai-tawhiti [Tamatea from afar] and Tamatea-pokai-whenua [Tamatea who travelled over the land], are considered by many authorities to belong to this ancestor: they believe, that is, that the one man possessed all of these names. Others assert that the extended names are employed in order to distinguish between several men who all bore the name Tamatea.

In a number of stories Tamatea is associated in one way and another with fire, which in some special sense is his possession. In many regions he is believed to have burnt the undergrowth he found on his arrival so as to prepare the land for his descendants.

In the South Island story, after the *Tākitimu* had been wrecked in the far south and turned into a mountain range, Tamatea walked along the eastern coastline creating landmarks as he went. Many of these landmarks are marked by his fire, such as an island in Foveaux Strait (its English name is Green Island) which is called 'Tamatea's firestick' [Te Kauati a Tamatea].

Tama-te-kapua
Captain of *Te Arawa*

In the homeland of Hawaiki, Tama-te-kapua and his younger brother Whakatūria became involved in a struggle between their father, Hou-mai-tawhiti, and the great rangatira Uenuku. Eventually this led to Tama-te-kapua's migration to Aotearoa as captain of *Te Arawa*.

The trouble began when Uenuku was suffering from a boil, and Hou-mai-tawhiti's dog Pōtaka-tawhiti was seen eating the discarded dressings – a dreadful insult, equivalent to eating Uenuku himself. Naturally Uenuku and his son, Toi-te-huatahi, killed the dog and ate it. Then Hou's sons, Tama-te-kapua and Whakatūria, went searching for the dog, calling as they went, and the dog howled back from inside Toi's stomach.

Hou had now been insulted as well, through his dog's being eaten. So

Tama-te-kapua and Whakatūria retaliated by stealing fruit from a tree owned by Uenuku. That led to further trouble, with Tama-te-kapua having to rescue Whakatūria from Uenuku and his men. A battle followed, and although Uenuku was defeated, Tama-te-kapua decided it was time to seek a new home. A waka was built, its crew were chosen, and they made their preparations.

It was known already that Tama-te-kapua was a bold resourceful man who did not hesitate to take what he wanted. On the voyage his character was further revealed. First, when *Te Arawa* was ready to sail, Tama persuaded the powerful tohunga Ngātoro-i-rangi to board the vessel with his wife Kea-roa so that the two of them could perform the ceremony to remove the ship's tapu. As soon as they came on board the anchor was raised, the sails were spread, the ship put out to sea – and Ngātoro realised too late that they had been kidnapped.

At the same time Tama-te-kapua committed another theft. He wanted the wife and property of a man named Ruaeo, so at the last moment he sent Ruaeo back on a pretended errand. He then set sail without him, carrying off his wife and possessions. (He did not know that Ruaeo would find his own way across the water and be waiting for him in Aotearoa, seeking revenge.)

On the voyage itself there was a further theft, which nearly proved fatal. Not content with having stolen Ngātoro-i-rangi, Tama-te-kapua decided to steal his wife, Kea-roa. While Ngātoro was elsewhere in the vessel, Tama-te-kapua took her by force. But Kea-roa told her husband what had happened, and the angry tohunga determined to destroy their ship. Only at the last moment was he persuaded to relent.

When *Te Arawa* arrived at Maketū, Tama-te-kapua found Ruaeo already there. Challenged to a dual, he suffered a humiliating defeat.

Afterwards the crew of *Te Arawa* spread out through the land. Tama-te-kapua lived at Maketū, then later went to live near the Moehau Range. When he died he was laid to rest on the summit of that mountain.

His habit of helping himself was recalled in sayings, and sometimes attributed to his descendants. One such saying is: 'Tama's descendants are always stealing something or other.' [Ngā uri o Tama whānako roa ki te aha, ki te aha].

Tāminamina
An East Cape story

Once some girls went swimming in a freshwater pool. Everyone knew about Tāminamina, the taniwha there. The elders used to warn the children that if they went near his den, or drank nectar from the flowers on the pōhutukawa trees above, Tāminamina would swallow them or drag them down into the water.

But one of these girls, Mere, was not frightened. She did drink nectar from the pōhutukawa trees, and she was dragged down by Tāminamina. The water in the stream became very dark, and it was now deep everywhere, though there had been shallow places before. Kelp from far out to sea was afterwards seen floating there, though salt water does not reach that place.

Tāne
Creator of the world

The world is made up of Rangi the sky and Papa the earth, but it was their son Tāne who pushed them apart and gave the world its proper form. Unlike most of his brothers, Tāne was in the shape of a human man. Some say he rested his shoulders upon the earth and pushed Rangi up with his legs, others that he raised Rangi through the power of a ritual chant; either way, he then placed props beneath him. On the west coast of the North Island it is said that these props can still be seen; they are the tall trees.

Next, Tāne searched for lights to adorn his father. In different myths he acquires the heavenly bodies from different people; Ngāti Kahungunu, for instance, say the stars came from Wehi-nui-a-mamao. When Tāne had thrown up the stars, the Moon and the Sun, his father was beautiful at last.

According to some traditions Tāne then made a human male, named Tiki. More often we are told that he went looking for a human female and that at first, finding only females who were not human, he fathered plants, birds and insects. Later he made himself a woman, Hine-ahu-one, by shaping her from the soil of Hawaiki.

In some traditions, Tāne is believed to have brought down from the skies three baskets [kete] containing sacred knowledge. Sometimes too he receives a whatu kura, a sacred stone which enables him to maintain order on the land below.

Being the ancestor of the trees and birds, Tāne is present now in his descendants, so must be propitiated before a tree of importance is felled. Since houses and waka are made from trees, they too are Tāne. And birds singing loudly at dawn are 'Tāne's mouth' [Te waka o Tane].

Since the word tāne ordinarily means 'male, husband, lover,' Tāne's name is a personification, Male. In the myths relating to him, male energy is presented as having shaped the world and created the life forms that belong to the land. Every human man – every tāne – who fathered a child was re-enacting the occasion on which Tāne, having obtained a wife, fathered the first of his children.

Tāne-atu
Creator of landmarks

This ancestor of the peoples of Ngāti Awa and Tūhoe was a brother of Tōroa, who captained the *Mātaatua* on its voyage from Hawaiki. In Aotearoa, Tāne-atua and his wife, Hine-mataroa, had many children. While the four youngest were apparently human, the elder children are not human but are features of special significance in the landscape.

Soon after his arrival at Whakatāne, Tāne-atua set out to explore the country. He walked up the Whakatāne Valley then right on to the Huiarau Range, and as he went he placed some of his children in the mountains there. They are now tipua, uncanny beings that take the form of rivers, streams and unusually shaped rocks.

Far inland, on the summit of the tapu mountain Maungapōhatu, his child Rongo-te-māuriuri is a taniwha living in the red waters of a pond of the same name.

Tāne-atua himself is sometimes said to have been a taniwha. Two peoples in the region of the Rangitāiki River, Ngāti Hamua and Warahoe, trace descent from him.

Tangaroa
Father of the fish

Tangaroa is one of the sons of Rangi the sky and Papa the earth (or sometimes their grandson, and a son of Tāne). Sometimes he lives at first on the land, then escapes to the ocean when he and his brothers quarrel and go their different ways. His role as the father of the fish and other sea creatures is referred to in many sayings.

Land and sea were experienced by the Māori as opposed realms, and in many situations they saw conflict between them. So Tangaroa, whose realm is the ocean, is in many contexts the enemy of Tāne, who as the father of trees, birds and humans represents the land. Some authorities taught that their mutual antagonism was established in the beginning, after the separation of their parents. It was in any case apparent whenever men in waka (representatives of Tāne) ventured out on the dangerous ocean to catch Tangaroa's children. Before and after their expedition, they were careful to make offerings to Tangaroa.

Yet sometimes in ritual a person might be associated with Tangaroa in order to gain his powers. A man cutting down a tree (which was Tāne) might in a chant identify himself with Tangaroa in order to use Tangaroa's strength against the tree.

Tangaroa-piri-whare
A hidden spy

A house, being made from trees, was in a sense Tāne (since Tāne had fathered the trees and was identified with them), and a spy inside a house could therefore be associated with Tāne's opponent, Tangaroa. In the Waikato district, the name Tangaroa-piri-whare [Tangaroa who clings to houses] was given to an unfriendly person who, overhearing things said in a house at night, would make mischief by repeating them later.

Tangaroa's whatu kura
A stone of great power

In the traditions of the Whanganui region and some other areas, Tangaroa is the owner of a whatu kura, a small, highly tapu stone of great mana (often said to be red) which was given to him in the beginning by the gods. Through its power he keeps the sea in its proper place so that it does not overwhelm the land.

For other peoples again, 'Tangaroa's whatu kura' [te whatu kura a Tangaroa] is simply an expression expressing admiration for something of great value. In the South Island it might be used when speaking of the daughters of a rangatira.

In the southern Bay of Plenty, the people of Te Whānau-ā–Apanui have a tradition concerning a red tapu stone of this name which came from Hawaiki. In the beginning, a woman named Hine sent her two daughters, Hine-tītama and Hine-ahu-one, fishing by the shore. The girls cast their net into the sea, but all they caught was a red stone. After this happened several times they were frightened and ran to tell their mother.

When Hine heard they had thrown the stone away, she expressed her strong disapproval: 'That stone was your ancestor. Go back and try to catch it.'

The girls soon found the stone. Their mother examined it carefully and said, 'This is a great treasure. If it is properly carved, we will catch enormous quantities of fish with its assistance.'

She told them the stone must be carved in the shape of a phallus. This was done, then she sent them off fishing once more. On the beach the girls recited chants to Tangaroa, then cast their net. Immediately they caught 3,000 fish.

Tangaroa's whatu kura was later brought from Hawaiki. It became a mauri for sea fishing which was treasured by Te Whānau-ā-Apanui.

Tangotango
Father of the children of light

In the traditions of Ngāti Awa and related peoples, it is often said that the first parents, Rangi and Papa, had two sons, Tāne and Tangotango, and a daughter, Wainui [Great waters]. Tāne is the father of trees, birds and humans, Tangotango is the origin of the alternation of day and night, and Wainui is the mother of water.

Tangotango made Wainui his wife and they had six children. These were Te Rā [The sun], Te Marama [The moon], Ngā Whetū [The stars], Te Hīnātore [Phosphorescence], Te Pari-kiokio [Kiokio fern cliffs], and Hine-rauāmoa [Moa plume woman]. Together they are known as Te Whānau Mārama [The children of light].

When Tāne saw how brightly the children shone, he asked his younger brother Tangotango to give him a child to light the world – because all was dark. He obtained one child after another, and he placed The Stars and The Moon in the sky. But he insisted on having The Sun as well.

Tangotango was very angry when he realised his elder brother wanted all his children, and he sent The Sun to destroy him. Tāne warded off The Sun's fierce rays and thrust Rangi, the sky, further up so that the heat would not destroy the people on the earth. And Tangotango's three eldest children, The Stars, The Moon and The Sun, now live in the sky. They are not subject to death like those who live below.

Taniwha
Spirits in the water

These beings live in the ocean and the inland waters, and some can move through the earth. Most are associated with humans, because every people have a taniwha of their own. Many famous taniwha arrived from Hawaiki, generally as guardians of ancestral waka, then settled down in Aotearoa with the descendants of the crew of the vessel they had escorted. Other taniwha are of unknown origin.

In the beginning, some taniwha created harbours by opening up channels to the sea. Others have caused landslides, especially by lakes and rivers.

There are many stories of heroic battles with taniwha, on the land and in the water. Often these struggles occurred soon after the settlement of Aotearoa, usually after a taniwha had attacked and devoured persons who belonged to a people with whom it had no connection. Always the humans win. Sometimes the taniwha's bones, turned to rock, can still be seen.

But when taniwha were respected they usually behaved well to their own people. Their dens were in deep pools in rivers, or dark caves, or places where there were strong currents or dangerous breakers, and travellers avoided these places when possible. If they had to pass the taniwha's den or wanted to go fishing nearby, they were careful to make a propitiatory offering, often of a green twig, and to recite the appropriate chant.

When all went well, taniwha were guardians of their people. They warned of the approach of enemies, communicating their messages to the tohunga who was their medium. They received offerings, often of the first kūmara and taro to be harvested and the first birds and fish to be caught in season. Because of their role as guardians they watched vigilantly to ensure that their people respected the tapu restrictions imposed upon them, and any violation of tapu was sure to be punished. Sometimes they drowned people, but on other occasions they saved persons from drowning.

On the ocean, taniwha often appear in the form of a whale or large shark. In rivers and lakes they may be as large as a whale, but look more or less like a gecko or tuatara; some have a row of spines down their backs, like male tuatara. Many can assume the form of a floating log, which may behave in an unusual way.

A man who had been associated with taniwha might become a taniwha after his death; this happened for instance to Te Tahi-o-te-rangi, who had been a medium of the taniwha and had been rescued by them. Another early ancestor, Tūheitia, became a taniwha after drowning, though with no prior association.

Then there were Hine-kōrako, a female taniwha who married a human man, and Pānia, a woman from the sea whose short-lived marriage to a human produced a son who later became a taniwha. There were relationships of many kinds.

Tapu and noa
Sacred and profane

Traditionally, Māori life was organised in all its aspects through the intricate interplay of two states of being, tapu and noa, which were complementary and of equal importance. In numerous contexts a person, place or thing would be said to be tapu or noa.

The word tapu indicates that the tapu person, place or object cannot be freely approached, that restrictions have been placed upon access; in many contexts it means 'restricted, forbidden' or 'sacred'. The word noa indicates unrestricted access and can generally be understood as 'ordinary, everyday, common, profane'.

Since nothing in Māori life and experience was secular – beyond the reach of religious thought and practice – noa cannot be translated as 'secular'. The noa, or profane, was a powerful counterbalance to the tapu, or sacred, and as such it was an essential element in daily life, ritual and thought.

Tapu restrictions were imposed for religious, social and political reasons, so varied greatly. Basically such a restriction marked the importance of a person or other entity by setting them apart from indiscriminate contact with others; it might also serve to protect a resource or property, or to focus attention on important undertakings. Atua were extremely tapu, and so were tipua and other supernatural beings. Tohunga, because of their relationship with atua and their tapu knowledge, were highly tapu. Rangatira were tapu as a consequence of their rank, with restrictions being observed to a greater or lesser degree in accordance with their precise status. The head of a tohunga or high-ranking person was extremely tapu. All the property of such a person was tapu (and therefore safe from thieves).

A low-ranking person who unknowingly ate the food of an important man might, if he were informed of this, die of shock. Yet it was thought that a rangatira could be seriously at risk when his tapu was infringed, however accidentally, for his atua could be expected to punish him with illness or other disaster for allowing this to happen.

A tohunga or high-ranking person might impose a temporary tapu. This was often done to protect for a period a seasonal food resource. After a death by drowning it was (and sometimes still is) customary to declare a stretch of coastline tapu for a certain time, so that no-one can fish those waters. Anything to do with the death of a person of rank involved severe tapu restrictions, as did such crucial events as birth and tattooing. People building a house, carving, adzing a waka or weaving a fine garment observed tapu restrictions, and warriors preparing for battle were placed under a severe tapu.

Intrinsically and in general, men were tapu and women were noa. In specific circumstances the situation was different; a woman might possess the tapu of high rank, while a low-ranking woman would be temporarily tapu after preparing a body for a funeral. In such cases the context of the tapu, therefore its meaning, was clear to all.

But just as women belonged with the earth and men with the sky, so women in themselves were essentially noa and men tapu. Woman's main responsibilities were seen as involving the continuance of life and the patterns of day-to-day existence, that which is noa, rather than the more specialised and isolated tasks of men. In the nature of things, everyday life tends to be taken for granted; yet the entire system of Māori life and thought depended upon the subtle interplay of these two states of being.

Frequently it was necessary to remove a state of tapu, or diminish it. Generally the complex rituals performed for this purpose required the presence of women – since they were noa – and food, especially cooked food, which was destructive of tapu. After a new house had been completed, its tapu had to be partly removed so that it would be safe for people to use; although the mana of the house required that some tapu remain, as the atua would otherwise desert it. The occupants of the house would respect the house's remaining tapu by observing the usual restrictions, such as the rule that there must be no eating inside.

A woman's presence is still required at the ceremonial opening of a meeting house, and out of respect for the house people still refrain from eating inside it.

Tāpui-kākahu
Owner of an heirloom

This ancestor of the people of Te Whakatōhea lived at Waiaua in the Ōpōtiki district. He was the owner of a treasured heirloom, a greenstone kahawai lure inlaid with pāua, and when he was fishing one day this fish hook was carried off by a big kahawai. So he went ashore, very unhappy at its loss, put on his precious dogtail cloak, and started following the school of kahawai as they moved across the surface of the sea. He ran along the coast, knowing they would be heading for the mouth of the Mōtū River, because that is the source of all the kahawai in the land.

At last he came to Maraenui, on the Mōtū. There he found the people of Te Whānau-ā-Apanui netting the kahawai. The women were gutting the fish, and soon one of them found the greenstone fish hook. She cried out and held it up, and Tāpui-kākahu told the woman why he had come. She gave him the fish hook, and in return he presented her with his dogtail cloak. Having regained his treasure, he then set out on the long journey back to Waiaua.

Tara
Founder of Ngāi Tara

Ngāi Tara, an early people in the far south of the North Island, traced their descent to Tara, who was born at Te Matau a Māui (the Cape Kidnappers region). Tara's father, Whātonga, had arrived from Hawaiki on the *Kurahaupō*.

Tara lived first at Te Aute, then moved south and settled by the wide stretch of water which his wife, Te Umu-roimata, named in his honour Te Whanga-nui-a-Tara [Tara's great harbour]; its English name is now

Wellington Harbour. His people's main pā there was Te Whetūkairangi, on the high ridge now known as Seatown Heights.

By the nineteenth century if not before, Tara's descendants had intermarried with other peoples to such an extent that they no longer used the name Ngāi Tara. In Te Whanga-nui-a-Tara and Porirua they merged with Ngāti Ira. In the Wairarapa they became a branch of Rangitāne.

Tara-ao and Karewa
Rival rangatira

In the southern Waikato, Tara-ao lived in the interior near Mount Kakepuku and Karewa lived on the western shore. Each man was married to the other's sister.

One day they quarrelled and parted in anger. So then Tara-ao went to steal Karewa's patu, carrying his own one with him; his patu had a plaited thong and Karewa's had a thong of dogskin. He approached under cover of darkness and found Karewa and his wife snoring in their house; the thong of Karewa's patu was looped right up by his armpit, with the patu pillowing their heads. Tara-ao boldly lifted their heads and took the patu, then to show what he had done he put his own one in its place.

Next morning as Karewa went to eat, his wife looked at the patu he was holding and she saw it belonged to Tara-ao. She cried out in dismay, and Karewa was greatly shamed to see that Tara-ao had had him at his mercy and spared his life. Because of this insult he summoned an army and set out to fight him.

Meanwhile Tara-ao and his people had been building a pā, with a long tunnel that could take them to safety if necessary. When Karewa besieged the pā, the armies fought through the night and Tara-ao and his warriors were hard pressed. Just before dawn they entered their tunnel, leaving Tara-ao's wife, Karewa's sister, sitting on the cover.

Karewa came running into the pā but couldn't find his enemies – then while he was still searching, Tara-ao's trumpet sounded in the distance. The woman called to Karewa, 'That's your brother-in-law who's escaped, sounding that trumpet there!'

When Karewa found the tunnel he was furious, but what could he do? Because Tara-ao was gone. He chased him, but couldn't catch him. Tara-ao made a new home in the north, and afterwards his wife went and lived with him once more.

Tara-i-whenua-kura
A happy outcome

Often this is the name of a great victory won by the people with whom the listeners are identifying. In one such tradition, set in the Tauranga region, the tohunga Ngātoro-i-rangi and his men overwhelm warriors led by Manaia.

On the west coast of the North Island there is a different story. A young man, Monoa, is pursued by enemies and attempts to conceal himself in flocks of birds; finally he manages to hide among a flock of terns. This occasion becomes known as Te Tara-i-whenua-kura, or (as the expression must have been understood in this context) 'The terns of the crimson land'.

In a Ngāti Porou chant believed to ensure possession of a treasured object, this property is personified as Tara-i-whenua-kura.

As the expression moved from one region to another it changed its meaning, but always referred to a much desired outcome.

Tara-ki-uta and Tara-ki-tai
Murdered twins

In Tūranga-nui (the Gisborne region), a rangatira named Rākai-hiku-roa received much tribute from the local people. His eldest son, Tūpurupuru, was also the recipient of gifts of food and valuable possessions. But then the flow of gifts lessened, and Rākai-hiku-roa became aware that they were being presented instead to the twin sons of his cousin Kahutapere. These boys, Tara-ki-uta and Tara-ki-tai, had become very popular and the people were now regarding them rather than Tūpurupuru as their future leaders.

Rākai-hiku-roa viewed this as an insult and sought revenge. On a visit to Kahutapere's pā he saw the twins whipping their tops, and as the tops spun past he knocked them into a kūmara pit. When the boys went down to retrieve their tops he killed them and hid their bodies.

Finding his sons missing, Kahutapere summoned his tohunga. To discover the murderer the tohunga sent up a kite, reciting chants to empower it, and the kite flew straight across a valley to the hill where Rākai-hiku-roa had his pā. When it hung motionless above Rākai-hiku-roa's house, it was known that he had killed the boys.

Afterwards Kahutapere and his allies attacked Rākai-hiku-roa's pā, killed his son Tūpurupuru, and forced Rākai-hiku-roa and his followers to migrate southwards from Tūranga. After much fighting these people settled at Te Wairoa (Wairoa) and Heretaunga (Hawke's Bay).

Taramainuku
The owner of a net

Some say this man came from Hawaiki on *Te Arawa*, others that he was a grandson of Tama-te-kapua and born in Aotearoa. He was a great fisherman, and his enormous seine net can be seen in a number of places.

In the Tāmaki region, dangerous rocks at the entrance to the Manukau Harbour are 'Taramainuku's seine net' [Te Kupenga-o-Taramainuku] and the islands of the Waitematā Harbour are its floats. In Heretaunga (Hawke's Bay), the posts to which the net was fastened are two high rocky pinnacles. To the Tūhoe people the entire Milky Way was his net.

Taranga
Māui's mother

The trickster hero Māui began life as a foetus that his mother, Taranga, threw into the sea after a miscarriage – or, in other versions of the myth, that she put in a bush-lawyer vine, or placed in the cave that held the bones of his ancestors. But Māui miraculously survived, grew up, and returned to his family. At first his mother did not recognise him, but then she welcomed him.

Every day Taranga disappeared at dawn. Māui wanted to know where she went, and to slow her departure he hid her clothes one night. She searched in vain for her skirt, and eventually fled without it.

Looking around the door, Māui saw his mother pull a clump of sedge from the ground and enter a hidden passage that went down under the ground. So he turned himself into a pigeon and flew down after her. (The pigeon's beautiful plumage is sometimes said to be Taranga's skirt, which Māui wore in order to achieve this transformation.)

Down below the disguised Māui made himself known to his mother, who greeted him with affection.

Māui's full name is Māui-tikitiki-o-Taranga [Māui the girdle of Taranga]; this is said by one narrator to recall Māui's origin in blood from

Taranga's tikitiki, or girdle. The place under the ground to which mother and son go is not Night [Te Pō], home of the dead; it appears to be another region down there which is normally unreachable.

Tarawhata
Owner of a supernatural dog

This man came from Hawaiki with a dog that had special powers. Some say he arrived on the *Mangarara*, which brought ancestors of Ngāti Porou to East Cape. Near the shore the dog jumped overboard, and kicked so hard it raised waves which wrecked the waka. Afterwards the creature turned into a cliff on the nearby island of Whanga-o-keno. In this form it remained dangerous; on one occasion its piercing gaze turned a woman to stone.

Others say that Tarawhata and his dog came on *Mātaatua*, and that the dog is now a rock with uncanny powers, a tipua, in the Whakatāne River near Pūkareao. It is also claimed that the two of them arrived on *Te Arawa*, and that at Tauranga the dog leapt from the waka, Tarawhata followed, and they swam ashore.

Taro
A favourite food

Several varieties of taro were grown for their starchy corms and the thick succulent stems of the leaves. The plants were not irrigated as often in tropical Polynesia, but were grown in warm parts of the country in rich damp soil, often by streams, with an upper layer of sand or gravel to warm the ground.

They were not very productive in terms of time and effort, so were a luxury reserved mostly for distinguished visitors. In certain ceremonies, such as the naming of a newborn child of rank, they formed a ritual meal. Sometimes at a funeral a seed taro would be placed in each hand so that the person would have food down in Te Rēinga.

Tautini-awhitia
A voyage to find a father

There was a woman who became pregnant and had a craving for birds, so her husband went off bird-spearing. He came back with a huia and a white heron, but the woman did not eat these birds. She kept them as pets.

Then the husband left the woman and returned to his own home. She stayed there, and gave birth to her son, Tautini-awhitia. When this boy grew big he asked his mother about his father and she told him where he was living. He made the voyage by magical means, sailing in the seedpod of a rewarewa tree.

At his father's village he was treated like a slave and sent to the cookhouse, because no one knew who he was. So he went into the forest and caught two birds, a huia and a white heron. He taught those birds to speak, then that night he went to the house and found the people asleep and snoring. He thrust in his birds, putting their supplejack cage in the ashes of the fire.

The huia called, 'The fire is not burning, it is dark, dark, dark!'

The white heron called, 'The fire is not burning, light shines!'

The people cried out in amazement at these wise birds. Then the boy's father stood up and said, 'This boy is my son, because these are the birds for which his mother longed.'

He wept over his son, and at daybreak he performed the tohi ceremony which acknowledged the boy's paternity and dedicated him to his future life.

The white heron and the huia were rare, treasured, tapu birds. Since the white heron in some contexts symbolised the male and the huia the female, the woman's pets together represented the child of unknown sex whom she was to have.

Tautoru
Three bright stars

The English name for this row of three stars is Orion's Belt. Along with another row of three stars nearby (Orion's Sword), it was often known to the Māori as 'Māui's handle' [Te Kakau a Māui] – the idea being that these six stars are the bent handle of an adze belonging to the trickster Māui.

Sometimes the two rows of stars were thought instead to be a bird-snare, of the kind that was baited with a rātā flower. This flower was the beautiful star Puanga (Rigel).

Tautoru was associated with the third month of the year (August-September) and indicated the time when the kūmara should be planted. As well it marked the approach of dawn.

Tāwera
The morning star

Before dawn the rising of Tāwera (Venus) in the eastern sky told restless sleepers that daylight would soon come, and his bright presence was greeted with songs and sayings. Another name for him is Kōpū.

Tāwhaki
A journey to the skies

Tāwhaki's place in the genealogies comes quite soon after the creation of the world. His main exploit is to climb to the skies. Being very handsome, he is loved by many women. Often he avenges his father's death.

On the East Coast, the Ngāti Porou story is that Tāwhaki and his younger brother Karihi set out to visit their grandmother, Whaitiri, in the sky. After overcoming enemies they began their climb. Karihi fell and died, but Tāwhaki was successful.

In the sky he found his grandmother, Whaitiri. She was blind, and she was sitting counting a pile of twelve taro. Tāwhaki tricked her by taking away her taro, one by one, then restored her sight by giving her the eyes of Karihi, his younger brother who had died. Whaitiri gave him one of her grand-daughters, Maikuku-mākaka, as his wife, and for a time Tāwhaki lived with them there.

But then he broke a prohibition: despite a warning he slept with his wife in the open, outside their house. This was too casual a way to treat a married woman, and the wife's relatives punished him by taking her up to a higher sky. Tāwhaki attempted to fly up, first on a kite and then as a hawk. But Tama-i-waho, a demonic being in the highest sky, cut off one of his wings, and Tāwhaki fell and died.

On the west coast of the North Island, Tāwhaki has two evil uncles, Punga and Karihi, whose children are sharks, dogfish and reptiles. These ugly offspring are jealous of their handsome cousin Tāwhaki, and they kill him. Tāwhaki, though, comes to life once more, and he sets out to climb to the sky in search of his grandmother Whaitiri. His uncle Karihi tries to accompany him, but fails.

Tāwhaki climbs up to the tenth of the skies, finds Whaitiri and restores her sight. He then avenges himself upon his murderous uncles by casting into the sea their children, the sharks and dogfish. That is why they live there now.

In the South Island, the first part of Tāwhaki's journey is not to the sky but across the ocean, and he mounts to the skies to avenge the murder of his father, Hemā, who has been killed by Te Whānau-a-Punga [Punga's family]. These include not only dogfish and sharks but the different kinds of seals encountered in the south, and whales as well. These large and sometimes dangerous marine mammals are the enemies that are thrust down from the skies and assume their proper place in the ocean.

In some parts of the country at least, Tāwhaki in certain respects prepares the way for human tohunga. Some South Island accounts have him receiving a knowledge of ritual chants [karakia] from Tama-i-waho in the highest sky; in another South Island text, he teaches ritual chants to tohunga; in yet another, he gains the first whatu (or whatu kura) from the sky.

Tohunga of importance were thought to be able to make the thunder sound, and they had this power, it was believed, because the thunder had obeyed Tāwhaki when he had called upon it to resound. Lightning, too, had flashed from Tāwhaki's armpits in token of his powers.

Tāwhaki's action in healing Whaitiri's eyes made him an appropriate role model for tohunga. As well, he was directly approached for assistance in healing.

On the west coast of the North Island, where he was regarded as 'a diefied man', offerings were made to him in a re-enactment of the scene in which Tāwhaki took Whaitiri's taro.

Tāwhirimātea
Father of the winds

This man is usually regarded as a son of Rangi the sky and Papa the earth. In an Arawa account, he quarrelled with his brothers when they resolved to separate their parents, and when Rangi was pushed upwards he followed him to the realms above. From there he continues to attack his brothers, sending down winds and storms.

It is usually believed that all the winds are his offspring, though some say that gales are his children and ordinary winds the children of Raka-maomao. The larger stars are also thought sometimes to be children of Tāwhirimātea.

Sometimes he is a son of Tāne, and grandson of Rangi and Papa.

Te Akē

A story of revenge

Te Akē and his people lived on the shores of the Akaroa Harbour some 200 years ago. When his beautiful daughter, Hineao, was killed through sorcery by a neighbouring rangatira, Turaki-pō, whom she had refused to marry, Te Akē travelled north to acquire a knowledge of sorcery from a great tohunga, Tautini. In response to his presents he was given powerful chants.

It was summer when he returned home, the time when the inland peoples visited the shore to fish and gather shellfish. Turaki-pō's people were camped on the coast in a cavern in the great rock known as Tuawera (Cave Rock, at Sumner). Seated on cliffs near his home and looking across the water at his enemies in the far distance, Te Akē recited a long chant to raise Tangaroa and all the other powers of the deep.

In the morning the people in the fishing camps woke to find a sperm whale, with seagulls hovering above, stranded on a sandbank near the shore. Greatly excited, they feasted upon the meat. Only Turaki-pō did not join in the celebrations. The previous night he had had an ominous dream, and he now had a presentiment of disaster. Saying nothing, he took the smallest of the waka and set out for his home. There he recited chants to avert sorcery.

Next morning Turaki-pō's people lay dead around their camp fires, destroyed by the terrible tapu of the whale's body. Te Akē had gained his revenge; for while it was a pity that Turaki-pō himself had not died, it was appropriate that his people should suffer for his misdeeds. From this time on, Tuawera Rock was shunned by all. It was a tapu place where spirits whistled in the night.

Te Aoputaputa
A lover's magic

Some twenty generations ago a young rangatira, Tahito-kura, lived on Titirangi Hill in Tūranga (the Gisborne district). On a visit to Ōpōtiki, far to the north, he fell in love with Te Aoputaputa, but she rejected him.

Back home, he decided to win her through magic. He made a neck pendant and cord, steeped them in scented oil, and placed them inside a ngāruru shell. He recited a chant to make Te Aoputaputa love him and seek him out, then he told the shell to go to Ōpape Beach and he threw it into the ocean.

The shell moved along the coast until it came to Ōpape, near Ōpōtiki. Te Aoputaputa was there, as Tahito had known she would be. She was diving for pāua with a group of women, but all she could see was this ngāruru shell. She threw the shell away and went somewhere else, but still it followed. In the end she took it to the beach. Then she noticed the pendant inside and put it around her neck. At once she thought of Tahito and she loved him.

So Te Aoputaputa walked alone through the forests and mountains from Ōpōtiki to Tūranga, and there she found Tahito and married him. Many peoples on the East Coast are descended from these two.

Te Ara Tāwhao
A voyage to gain the kūmara

In the early times Toi lived with his people at Whakatāne, in a pā named Te Kapu-o-te-rangi on a high hill above the sea. The only vegetable foods they knew were fernroot and other wild plants.

One morning Toi's daughter discovered on the shore two strangers who had come from the homeland of Hawaiki. These men, Hoake (or Hoaki) and his younger brother Taukata, had floated all the way on a piece of pumice stone. She led them to the pā and her people offered them a meal of fernroot.

The men accepted this but did not like it, and ate with difficulty. Then Taukata untied his carry-belt and produced some dried kūmara he had brought with him. He mixed it with water and offered it to his hosts, who were delighted with this new food.

When Toi asked Hoake and Taukata how he could obtain the kūmara, they told him he must construct a ship and sail to Hawaiki. Toi did not know how to do this, but was advised by the two brothers. They told him that a tōtara log, washed up on the shore, would be their waka.

Because of its origin, Toi's vessel was named *Te Ara Tāwhao* [The driftwood path]. It reached Hawaiki under the captaincy, it is sometimes said, of Toi's son Tama-ki-Hikurangi, and the crew obtained the kūmara there. They left their vessel in Hawaiki and later sailed back to Aotearoa in the *Mātaatua*.

Te Ara-tukutuku
A son's revenge

Te Ara-tukutuku was a human woman whose son, Te Ihi, had become a taniwha. While visiting the pā at Ōhinemutu, by Lake Rotorua, she was insulted by some women there, and she called upon her son to revenge her. In response the taniwha caused half of the pā to sink down into the lake.

Later, back among her people at Taupō, Te Ara-tukutuku was murdered by men who had accused her of sorcery. Again her son acted on her behalf, destroying two pā beside Lake Taupō by sending them down into the water.

Te Arawa
Waka of the Arawa peoples

A war in Hawaiki led to the voyage of *Te Arawa* to Aotearoa. This struggle began when the powerful rangatira Uenuku suffered from a boil, and the dog belonging to another rangatira, Hou (or Hou-mai-tawhiti), found the discarded dressings and ate them. To avenge this terrible insult, Uenuku and his son Toi killed the animal and ate it.

Hou's sons, Tama-te-kapua and Whakatūria, went searching for the dog and discovered its fate. To revenge themselves, they went by night on stilts to steal fruit from a tree owned by Uenuku. Eventually they were caught; Tama-te-kapua escaped, but Whakatūria was captured and hung up inside the roof of their enemies' house. Learning what had happened, Tama-te-kapua climbed the roof, made a hole in the thatch and spoke to his younger brother. He had a plan, and he told Whakatūria what to do.

So Whakatūria called down to his enemies and told them how badly they were dancing and how much better he could do. They gave him a chance to prove it and he danced his haka, leaping from one side of the house to the other. Presently he asked for the door to be opened so he could cool down. Then he danced again – and straight out through the doorway. Tama-te-kapua, sitting ready in the porch, fastened the door and window so the enemy could not follow.

But this led to fighting, and many were killed. In the end Tama-te-kapua decided it was time to go.

When *Te Arawa* had been constructed and lay ready, there was no tohunga to guide and protect the waka. So Tama-te-kapua resolved to take with him the great tohunga Ngātoro-i-rangi, who was about to travel on the *Tainui*. Some say Tama persuaded Ngātoro to join *Te Arawa*, others that he kidnapped him.

It is certain that Tama stole Whakaotirangi, the wife of Ruaeo. He did this by tricking Ruaeo into going back at the last moment to fetch an adze Tama claimed to have forgotten – then off they went without him, and Tama had the woman to himself.

During the voyage Tama, not satisfied with this, stole Ngātoro-i-rangi's wife Kea (or Kea-roa) as well. The enraged tohunga called up the winds and began to send *Te Arawa* down to destruction in the throat of Te Parata, the monster at the edge of the ocean. When the crew wept and cried as the vessel began to slide into the abyss, Ngātoro had pity on them and brought the ship back up.

They sailed on, and at last approached Rātānui, near Tikirau (Cape Runaway, on the East Coast). The rātā trees were in bloom, and when the voyagers saw the crimson flowers they threw their own red plumes into the water, thinking such things were freely available in the new land. Too late they discovered their mistake.

The vessel then sailed north, and finally landed at Maketū (in the Bay of Plenty). Some time later, a number of men set out to explore the country and lay claim to territory. Tama-te-kapua returned to Moehau, Tia went inland to the Taupō region, Hei lived by Mount Hikurangi (inland from Katikati), and Tua (or Tua-Rotorua) settled by Lake Rotorua, where he was later joined by Īhenga.

Ngātoro-i-rangi in his explorations revealed his great powers. He walked far inland to Tongariro, he climbed that mountain, and with the help of his two sisters from Hawaiki he lit the fires that burn there now.

The three of them then returned to Maketū, the sisters creating hot springs and mud pools on the way.

Some time later, *Te Arawa* was burnt by an enemy rangatira, Raumati, as it lay at Maketū. This dreadful crime was avenged by Hatupatu, a warrior with extraordinary powers.

Te Atarahi
The man who came back

This man died, and was buried. Then when summer came, and the month when the flax flowers open, he came up out of his grave and went around on the flax flowers drinking their nectar; he perched up there like a bird. All his hair had fallen out. There was only his head and his bones.

Some people came along, drinking from the flax flowers, and they saw the dead man. They were terrified and ran home. Then the others went to look, and asked who it could be. They visited the graves and saw that Te Atarahi's grave was empty.

They went back and found him still on the flax flowers. They chased him, and he jumped into some fern. Then the tohunga recited chants, and he slipped from the fern to the ground. They led him to the tūāhu, and his flesh returned; soon he again took on the appearance of a man. He was given food and he recovered.

When he died a second time, that was the end.

Te Awhiorangi
The mana of all the adzes

The most ancient of the heirlooms brought from Hawaiki was an adze called Te Awhiorangi [The sky-encircler]. It was the mana, the source of power, of all the adzes in the world, their spiritual prototype.

In the traditions of southern Taranaki this adze was made by Ngahue and given to Tāne, who used it to cut the poles which he placed between his parents Rangi and Papa. Among Ngāti Kahungunu on the East Coast, it is asserted that Te Awhiorangi was brought to Aotearoa by Tamatea, captain of the *Tākitimu*, and that on the ocean he used it to cut through the waves of a storm sent by enemies to bar the way.

Te Hōkioi
A great bird

The world's largest eagle, with a wingspan of up to three metres and talons wider than a tiger's claws, once inhabited the South Island and the southern half of the North Island. The New Zealand eagle preyed upon big, flightless birds such as moa and takahē. It became extinct when its food supply dwindled, about five hundred years ago.

Stories in Māori tradition about a great bird named Te Hōkioi may be based partly upon information about this eagle which had been passed down and reinterpreted. One Māori authority wrote that Te Hōkioi was a very large hawk that lived on the tops of mountains, another that it stayed always in the sky and was a descendant of the star Rehua. It was sometimes thought a bad omen to see or hear it, no doubt because of its association with warfare.

Some said it was seen only in flight, some that it was never seen because it always flew at night, and others that it was not visible to 'the multitude' but only to those of high birth. On rare occasions it could be heard loudly calling its name: 'Hōkioi, Hōkioi, hū!'

Te Hono-i-wairua
The meeting-place of wairua

Orators and poets in many parts of the country trace their people's beginnings to Tawhiti-nui [Great distance], Tawhiti-roa [Long distance], Tawhiti-pāmamao [Far distance] and Te Hono-i-wairua [The meeting of wairua].

The last of these is regarded as a land of origin to which the wairua return after death. Some say it is in a land known as Irihia that lies across the ocean.

Te Huhuti and Te Whatuiāpiti
A love story

Near the end of the seventeenth century a young rangatira named Te Whatuiāpiti was living on an island in Te Roto-a-Tara, a lake in southern Heretaunga (Hawke's Bay). While visiting a pā some distance away he met Te Huhuti, the daughter of the rangatira there, and they fell in love.

Before leaving for his home, Te Whatuiāpiti told Te Huhuti to follow. She set off alone, she came at night to the shore of the lake, and she boldly swam across.

As she reached the island she was found by Te Whatuiāpiti's mother. Some say the mother was angry at first because she had been told nothing of this, but that later there was a reconciliation. The lovers soon married, and had many descendants.

Te Ihi
A powerful taniwha

Te Ihi began life as a man, then one day he dived from a waka into the waters of Lake Taupō and was lost to sight. He was thought drowned, but when he surfaced in Lake Rotorua it was seen that he had become a taniwha. In appearance he is like a giant reptile. Great waves are a sign of his presence.

Te Kahureremoa
A journey to find a husband

This woman was the daughter of Pāka, a rangatira living at Wharekawa by the Hauraki Gulf. She lived, it seems, in the early seventeenth century.

Her father wanted her to marry a neighbouring rangatira, but she would not agree. Later this suitor arrived with a gift of fish, and Te Kahureremoa ran to get one for herself. But Pāka angrily sent her away, saying that since she had refused the man she could not have any of his fish.

Te Kahureremoa was deeply shamed. She left the basket of fish, went inside her house and wept. Then she made up her mind that she would leave her father and her people, and would have Takakōpiri as her husband. This man was a rangatira of Waitaha, an Arawa people living at Te Puke. He was a distant relative, and she had seen him when he had visited Hauraki; she knew him to be a good-looking man of wealth and position.

So she set off that night, running away with her slave; by the time her people found them gone, they were so far ahead they could not be caught.

They made their way along the shore of the Hauraki Gulf as far as the Waihou River, then boarded a passing waka owned by people who had recognised her. She went upriver to Te Raupa, spent a night there, then climbed the Kaimai Ranges. Looking down she saw Katikati and Tauranga, and far in the distance the lands of Takakōpiri.

After passing through Katikati and Te Wairoa, Te Kahureremoa and her attendant reached Te Puke. She found Takakōpiri, and she married him. Their marriage linked their two peoples and their daughter, Tūparahaki, became a famous ancestor.

Te Kāhui Tipua
A company of giants

These are tipua, beings with extraordinary powers; their name means 'The supernatural company'. They lived in a distant land known as Te Pātū-nui-o-Āio, then grew tired of their home and travelled to other islands. But they were not satisfied, and kept moving on. Even at Hawaiki the food did not please them, and they crossed over to Te Ika-a-Māui (The North Island). They got here by walking across the water. Their guide was a large white bird named Komakahua.

Soon they began quarrelling amongst themselves, so Komakahua took three of the most dangerous tipua over to Te Wai Pounamu (the South Island). Those he chose were Te Kārara-huarau (or Te Ngārara-huarau), a reptile with a human head; Te Pouākai, a huge bird; and Kōpūwai, who had a man's body and the head of a dog. In the south he found homes for them, well apart. Since Te Kārara-huarau was the worst of the three, Komakahua made his own home near his cave so he could watch what he did.

Te Kaiwhakaruaki
A giant reptile

Te Kaiwhakaruaki was a reptile living in the Te Parapara Stream at Tai-tapu (Golden Bay). This monster used to devour the travellers who approached his home. Finally their fate was discovered and an army under the leadership of Pōtoru went to fight him.

Among them was a valiant warrior of Ngāi Tahu who used to kill seals with his fist as his only weapon. This man now boasted, 'One blow of my fist, and he dies! Is he more powerful than the seals I kill with a single blow? How can he survive me?'

Pōtoru had planned an ambush, but the seal-killing warrior insisted that he must first have the opportunity to fight Te Kaiwhakaruaki. When all was ready he went forward alone.

He waded into the river and the reptile approached at once. The man struck the monster on the nose, twisting his head, then Te Kaiwhakaruaki came again, his mouth gaping wide. The warrior dealt another blow, but this time he missed the nose. His fist went straight into the reptile's mouth and he disappeared into its belly.

The army then attacked, and after a fierce battle Te Kaiwhakaruaki was killed. Inside his body they found human bones, and weapons and garments of every kind.

Te Māmaru
A northern vessel

This ship was first named the *Tinana*. Under the command of Tūmoana it sailed from Hawaiki to Ahipara, then many years later Tūmoana returned to Hawaiki, leaving behind his daughter Kahutianui.

The vessel was refitted and given a new name, *Te Māmaru*, then it sailed back under the captaincy of Tū-moana's nephew, Te Parata. This man built his pā at Rangiaohia and married Kahutianui. They became founding ancestors of Ngāti Kahu.

Te Mangōroa
The Milky Way

The Milky Way is often known as Te Mangōroa [The long shark]. Hāmiora Pio of Ngāti Āwa writes that 'the biggest company of people in the sky is Te Mangōroa. All these people travel together, they do not scatter. The fathers, mothers, elder and younger brothers, grandchildren (male and female), children, old men and cousins, all keep together. Their great task is to foretell the coming of day. Such is the Māori sign of the coming dawn – those people in the sky.'

At the approach of dawn, Te Mangōroa swings around in the sky and awaits the sun with his head towards the east. Some explain that he loves the sun because the sun is his younger brother.

Te Ngārara-huarau
An enemy of humans

A favourite story tells how a giant reptile kidnaps a woman, makes her his wife, then is attacked and killed by her people. One of the names given this monster, especially in the south, is Te Ngārara-huarau (or often, in the southern dialect, Te Kārara-huarau).

Generally the reptile, having captured the woman, tries to get accepted into human society. A woman living on Rangitoto (D'Urville Island) was kidnapped by Te Ngārara-huarau but eventually escaped; her brothers built a great house to hold the repulsive creature, then invited him to their village and burnt the house around him.

Usually the monster is male, but in one story a female reptile named Te Ngārara-huarau pursued a human man, Ruru-teina. The humans lured her into a house and she was burnt to death.

Te Niniko
A man with a fairy wife

When a fairy [patupaiarehe] woman saw this man dancing, she loved him. She would visit him in his house then disappear before dawn.

Te Niniko wanted to show his beautiful wife to his people, but she told him, 'You must wait till my child is born, otherwise you will never see me again.'

Te Niniko was too impatient. He did tell his people, and they advised him to stop up the chinks in the house so the fairy woman would not know the dawn was coming. He did this, then when the sun was high he pulled aside the door. The fairy woke to the light, ran outside and climbed to the top of the house. She sang a song of farewell to her husband, then a patch of mist came down and carried her off.

Te Parata
Origin of the tides

Te Parata, or Parata, is a giant sea-creature who lives in the deepest part of the ocean – or, some say, at the edge of the sky. The tides are caused by his breathing, which happens twice a day. He is often regarded as a son of Tangaroa, whose realm is the sea, though some believe him to be Tangaroa himself under a different name.

Te Pouākai
A giant bird

Often this is a single bird, though some writers tell of a pair of birds and their young. Sometimes the creature lives in Hawaiki, or a similar island, and is killed by two seafarers driven ashore in a storm. These men build a specially designed house and attack the bird from within it.

In other accounts Te Pouākai lives in Aotearoa. In the best known of these stories, one of the birds made its home on Tāwera (Mount Torlesse, highest peak in a range bordering the Canterbury Plains). This bird attacked the people living nearby, until at last a brave man named Ruru devised a plan. One night he led forty warriors to a place near the mountain and began to construct a house with a very strong framework but no thatch, just open spaces between the rafters. Every night they worked on this structure and soon it was finished. The men went inside, and Ruru set off to lure Te Pouākai.

At dawn he saw the enormous bird flying towards him. He ran, and reached the house just in time. Te Pouākai clawed at the roof, thrusting a foot between the rafters; some men were killed, but the others managed to cut the leg off. The furious bird thrust in the other foot, then one wing, then the other, and each time the same thing happened. Then the surviving warriors, Ruru among them, unfastened the door and clubbed the now helpless bird to death.

Stories about Te Pouākai seem to have been told mostly in the South Island. A giant bird of prey, the New Zealand eagle, once inhabited the South Island and the lower part of the North Island; it lived upon moa and other flightless birds and became extinct about the same time that they did, perhaps about 500 years ago. These stories may be based upon information about this bird which had been passed down and reinterpreted.

Te Pupū and Te Hoata
Origin of volcanic fire

Two sisters are the origin and personification of the supernatural [tipua] fire that creates volcanoes and thermal activity. Their fire was introduced to the country by the powerful tohunga Ngātoro-i-rangi (said to be their brother, or sometimes their descendant).

After arriving from Hawaiki on *Te Arawa*, this man set off with a slave to explore the country, and at Taupō he decided to climb Ngāuruhoe (which was traditionally regarded as part of Mount Tongariro). By the time they reached the summit, Ngātoro-i-rangi and his slave were in danger of freezing to death. So Ngātoro-i-rangi called with a voice like thunder to Te Pupū and Te Hoata, back in Hawaiki, and the sisters heard him and came at once.

On the way they rested on Whakaari (White Island, an active volcano), and there they lit a fire that is still burning. Then they made their way underground, with sparks from their fire becoming hot springs, geysers and mud pools. On Ngāuruhoe, Ngātoro-i-rangi seized the fire and hurled it into the crater. Afterwards the sisters returned to their home, creating more thermal activity as they went.

Te Rangihouhiri
Leader of a long migration

The people of Ngāi Te Rangi now belong to the Tauranga district. Their ancestors once lived near Ōpōtiki, far to the south, and like other peoples from that region they trace their origin to the arrival from Hawaiki of the *Mātaatua*.

After being defeated in battle they left the Ōpōtiki district for the east coast and sought shelter in a subordinate capacity with a section of Ngāti Porou at Whāngārā. When their numbers grew, the local people feared they were becoming too powerful and attacked them. Ngāti Houhiri (as they were then known) repulsed the attack, but soon afterwards left Whāngārā under the leadership of Te Rangihouhiri.

They migrated first to Ūawa (Tolaga Bay), then Te Kaha, then Tōrere, then back to the Ōpōtiki district. After another defeat they fought their way northwards along the Bay of Plenty and reached Maketū, which was occupied by the Tapuika people (a section of Te Arawa).

Ngāi Te Rangi, as they were now known, were offered land near Maketū and for a while they lived there peacefully. But after a series of battles (in one of which Te Rangihouhiri was killed), they abandoned Maketū for Tauranga. There they stormed the great pā at Mount Maunganui and overcame the two peoples in the region, Ngāti Ranginui and Waitaha. The Tauranga district became their home, and as always the fighting was followed by marriages between the two sides.

Te Rapuwai
An early people

In the South Island, Te Rapuwai were sometimes regarded as very early human inhabitants. Some people believed they had come up from the ground; others said they had arrived from Hawaiki on the *Uruao*, and that soon afterwards they had fought and overcome monsters, such as Kōpūwai, who preyed upon them.

Others again believed Te Rapuwai to have been giants, not humans, even when they agreed they had come on the *Uruao*.

Te Rēinga
The place of departure

The usual belief is that after death a person's wairua remains three days with the mourning relatives, then leaves for a destination which is known both as Te Rēinga [The leaping-place] and as Te Rerenga Wairua [The leaping-place of the wairua]. This barren promontory is in the far north-west of the North Island. Its English name is Cape Rēinga.

Some wairua make their way down the rivers, then travel by sea; others go by land. People in the far north were well aware of their presence. Some could hear on misty days the faint high singing of the wairua, and their chatter and laughter.

The ascent begins at the northern end of Te One Roa a Tōhē (Ninety Mile Beach). On Haumu, the headland above the beach, wairua from the two coasts and the inland districts meet, then set out along ridges in the interior. They climb the last ridge, which extends along the rocky cape; they go up Hiriki Hill, then down a steep slope to a precipitous cliff. An ancient stunted pōhutukawa tree clings to a cleft in the rock below; the wairua make their way to it, then down a hanging root (some say a branch).

From a platform of rock they watch the swirling seaweed that hides the watery cave beneath, and they leap when the waves have swept it aside.

The underworld itself, which lies below, is often known (like the approaches to it) as Te Rēinga; its other name is Night [Te Pō]. In one northern tradition the wairua enters a series of regions, becoming weaker as it passes through them.

But many believe that the wairua only visit the underworld, then afterwards go out over the ocean to the far homeland of Hawaiki. The strong currents around Te Rēinga take them to Manawa-tāwhi, largest of the islands known now as The Three Kings. The souls look back and weep once more, sending their greetings [mihi] for the last time to their relatives and the land, then they move on out towards Hawaiki.

These are the northern traditions, which naturally provide more geographical detail than those elsewhere. In most parts of the country the general idea of a journey north to Te Rēinga was accepted, and names such as Haumu are mentioned by poets. But in certain regions the beliefs were different. Sometimes it seems to have been thought that Te Rēinga, or Te Rerenga, lies close at hand and can be readily reached; sometimes there is a journey of a different sort.

Te Ririō
Guardian of Tongariro

The windswept plateau around Mounts Ruapehu, Ngāuruhoe and Tongariro was ruled by Te Ririō, with other atua. These spirits lived high on the mountains. They were sometimes spoken of as maero, being rather similar to humans but very hairy and with clawlike hands.

They punished infringements of the laws of tapu, and constantly watched the actions of travellers passing through the intensely tapu uplands near their homes. Many people in this wild region heard them shouting and singing, though they were visible only to those they carried off. People passing the mountains for the first time showed their respect for the spirits by shading their eyes with wreaths of leaves which prevented them from gazing at the tapu heights.

Te Rongorito
An opponent of strife

This woman, an important ancestor in the upper Waikato, lived in the valley of the Waipā River. She named her home Te Marae o Hine [The daughter's (or woman's) marae], and it became the centre of an area that was set apart as tapu. No strife occurred there and no war parties were permitted to enter. In times of war it became a place of refuge.

Te Ruahine
A source of fertility

Mythical voyagers cast upon the shores of Hawaiki, or some other strange island, often encounter an old woman living alone, or with younger women as her companions. This old woman's main role is to be in possession of fertility. Sometimes she is termed a ruahine (a word generally used of a woman who is probably old and certainly senior, and who participates in rituals in which her female powers are required, such as the removal of tapu). Sometimes instead the old woman's name in these myths is Te Ruahine [The ruahine], or an extended version of this name.

Hawaiki itself is traditionally the source of fertility, and similar ideas are often involved when the island is nameless or bears some other name. The presence only of women is indicative of the island's potential for fertility – one which the voyager actualises.

Māori mythology, like other mythologies, reflects in endless ways a male nervousness about women – who were an essential presence, greatly valued, yet potentially dangerous and, in some contexts, associated with death and Night [Te Pō]. The very fact that women have the power to give birth made for anxiety. Sometimes the old woman in these stories provides a man with kūmara or a wife, but on other occasions she is menacing and her possessions must be taken by force.

These myths seem to belong mainly to the South Island and the far south of the North Island. Usually they are set in Hawaiki or a similar island, but in a South Island version of the myth of Tāwhaki he encounters Te Ruahine-mata-morari in the sky.

Te Tahi-o-te-rangi
The tohunga who rode a whale

This tohunga belonged to a section of Ngāti Awa who were living at Whakatāne. His people blamed him for the floods that kept spoiling their crops, and they wanted to be rid of him. Knowing they could not shed the blood of a tohunga, they decided to go fishing for sharks near Whakaari (White Island) and leave him there to die. They did this, then sailed back to Whakatāne.

But Te Tahi did not die. He climbed a rock and called to the taniwha, and before long they floated up. He mounted their rangatira, Tūtara-kauika, and the great creatures swam towards the land. Soon they caught up with Ngāti Awa and the taniwha asked what they should do with them.

Te Tahi said, 'Let shame be their punishment.'

Ngāti Awa, returning, found Te Tahi on the shore. At first they could not believe he was Te Tahi, then they saw to their shame that it really was so.

When Te Tahi died and was buried, his taniwha friends came to fetch him. They carried him off and he is now a taniwha in the ocean. Sometimes he saves his descendants from drowning.

Te Waka-a-Raki
A cargo of stars

In South Island tradition, Te Waka-a-Raki [Raki's ship] is a very early waka that sailed to Aotearoa from an unknown land. Raki is the South Island equivalent of the northern name Rangi, so this man may be identified or associated with Rangi the sky father, but this is not known.

The crew were Te Tinitini-o-te-Para-rākau [The great multitudes of the Para-rākau]. Their ship made landfall at the northern end of the North Island, then its likeness was transferred to the sky. There it became Tama-rereti's ship.

This vessel brought the stars, which ever since have sent down their messages to people below.

Te Wera
A warrior who met his match

Te Wera, a famous warrior of Ngāi Tahu who was born in about 1730, led an expedition to Rakiura (Stewart Island) and easily conquered the few people of Ngāti Māmoe who were living there. But then he was threatened on the shore by an angry sea lion. Although Te Wera had never fled from human enemies, he did run now from this ferocious beast.

A saying recalls that 'Te Wera's enemy was a bull sea lion' [Te hoa kakari o Te Wera, he whakahao]. The implication is that everyone meets their match sooner or later.

Te Whare Kura
A great house in Hawaiki

In a Whanganui tradition, the peoples of Hawaiki used to assemble to discuss important matters in a great house, painted with red ochre and very tapu, which was known as Te Whare Kura [The crimson house]. The carved posts supporting this buildings were their ancestors.

The leaders of the different peoples were ranged inside in two great divisions, one led by the great rangatira Uenuku, famous for his oratory and wisdom, and the other by Maru, god of war. At first there was unity and accord, then the two sides quarrelled, and in the end they fought. The famous warrior Whakatau-pōtiki set fire to the building and a multitude perished in the flames.

From that early time in Hawaiki there has been no unity amongst human beings. Groups of people have ever since opposed each other.

Another writer says nothing about a struggle between two sides, claiming instead that Te Whare Kura was erected so that those inside could make offerings to Maru. And many people say that Whakatau-pōtiki burnt a different house, Te Tihi o Manōno.

These are mythical accounts. In reality, schools were held in tapu buildings for the instruction in esoteric knowledge of high-ranking youths. In some parts of the country, including the west coast, the expression referring to such a house of learning was Te Whare Kura.

Tia
An early Arawa explorer

After arriving from Hawaiki on *Te Arawa*, Tia set out from Maketū with Māka and other companions to explore the interior. Reaching the Waikato River, he followed it to its source in a great lake.

At Pākā, on the eastern shore, he saw a high rocky cliff that resembled a cloak of the kind he was wearing, a black and yellow garment known as a taupō. At the foot of this cliff he erected a tūāhu to propitiate the unknown gods there, and establish his claim to the district. He fastened his own taupō cloak to the tūāhu as an offering, and he called the region Taupō. He then continued along the shore, erecting more tūāhu at intervals.

Meanwhile the powerful tohunga Ngātoro-i-rangi, who had also come on *Te Arawa*, had arrived in the region and was himself erecting tūāhu. When he saw Tia's tūāhu by the cliff, he cunningly constructed his own tūāhu from old materials so it would seem he had the prior claim.

When the two men met, Tia was persuaded by the sight of the shrine that looked much older than his own. Leaving this region for Ngātoro-i-rangi, he went on to Tokaanu and settled there with his people.

Tia's son Tapuika became the founding ancestor of the Tapuika people in the Te Puke area.

Tieke-iti
A dancing thief

There were once two brothers, Tieke-iti [Little Tieke] and Tieke-rahi [Big Tieke]. These brothers behaved quite differently. The elder brother, Tieke-rahi, would go out fishing, while the younger one would go stealing kūmara.

One day the owners of the kūmara lay in wait for him, and when the thief was inside the storage pit they blocked the entrance and caught him. They were going to kill him, but Tieke-iti said, 'Wait, don't kill me till I've danced for you.'

Everyone agreed to this: 'Yes, yes!'

So he started to dance his haka. They admired his skill and allowed him to continue. All the time he danced further away, then he ran off and they couldn't catch him.

Tiki
Origin of sexuality

In some traditions, as on the East Coast, the first human is a woman whom Tāne creates (usually she is Hine-ahu-one). In other traditions, the first human made by Tāne is a man named Tiki. Sometimes Tāne then makes a wife for Tiki.

In other accounts again, it is Tiki himself who creates the first person. And some authorities bring these ideas together by saying that Tiki is Tāne's penis.

When Tiki makes the first human, as often on the west coast, he is sometimes regarded as a son of the first parents, Rangi and Papa. The person he makes is always male, and he does so, often, by mixing clay with his own blood.

As the maker of the first man, Tiki is the creator of all children born subsequently. As well he is mentioned in chants to heal broken bones (just as Tāne's name is used in such chants in other regions).

Always, though, it is Tiki who is the initiator of sexuality itself. Even when Tāne was believed to have made the first woman and had sex with her, love-making was Tiki's speciality. A woman poet in trouble for taking a lover might blame her predicament upon Tiki, since he had started it.

Timu-whakairia
A source of sacred knowledge

In Hawaiki, Ruawhārō and his younger brother, Tūpai, insulted the great rangatira Uenuku by taking for themselves the best fish in his men's net. After the angry fishermen retaliated by throwing the net over them, the brothers decided to ask their grandfather Timu-whakairia, the most powerful tohunga in Hawaiki, to teach them ritual chants that would enable them to revenge this injury.

Since they planned a voyage to Aotearoa (they later came on the *Tākitimu*), these men also wished to acquire the mauri of the whales, which Timu-whakairia possessed. These mauri took the form of two sacred pools and a great rock that held the life-force of all the whales in the ocean.

So Ruawhārō and Tūpai set out on their journey. On the way they found the old man's beautiful wife, Kapuarangi, working in her flax plantation. Forgetting their errand, the two men desired her and possessed her. And two pet birds belonging to Timu-whakairia saw this scene and flew to tell their master.

Since the men were his grandsons Timu-whakairia did not destroy them, but instead planned his revenge. When his visitors arrived he seated them upon fine mats and presented them with a large, delicious meal of a variety of pūpū [periwinkle] which has one drawback: this shellfish has an almost immediate purgative effect. Very soon disaster overcame the two men and the mats upon which they sat. Their shame was Timu-whakairia's revenge.

Further ordeals followed, then Timu-whakairia agreed to give Ruawhārō the ritual chants. He would not consent to teach Tūpai, considering that only the elder brother was worthy of instruction. But Tūpai eavesdropped outside the building, and according to one story he was able to repeat the chants when Ruawhārō at first failed to do so. Ruawhārō, however, eventually acquired the knowledge he needed.

Tinirau
Rangatira of the fish

This handsome man lived on Motu-tapu [Sacred island] or, it is sometimes said, in Hawaiki. He had power over all the fish in the ocean, especially the whales, and he had one particular pet whale named Tūtūnui. Generally in Tinirau's story there is an episode in which he permits a visitor (usually named Kae) to return home on the back of Tūtūnui.

Often Tinirau has a wife, Hine-te-iwaiwa (or Hina-uri). Having heard what a fine man he was, this woman swam through the ocean for many days to find him. She became his wife and presently had his son, Tūhuruhuru.

Kae, in these versions of the story, is a tohunga who visits the island to conduct the naming ceremony over Tūhuruhuru – or sometimes, instead, he is a rangatira present for the occasion. In versions where there is no wife or son, Kae may be cast up on the shore, or may come as a tohunga to heal Tinirau's illness.

Whatever the circumstances, Tinirau lends Kae his pet whale, warning that close to land the creature will shake himself and must then be allowed to return to the sea. But Kae abuses the trust placed in him. He remains seated on the whale's back until the tide ebbs and the great creature is stranded, then he and his people kill and eat him.

The appetising smell of the meat from the ovens is blown on the wind across the water, and Tinirau knows what has happened and plans his revenge. In some accounts he sends a war party, in others a party of women who must find Kae and bring him back. In both cases Kae is carried to Hawaiki, sound asleep, and wakes unsuspecting in Tinirau's house. There he is killed by Tinirau.

Tipua
Supernatural presences

Tipua, generally speaking, were beings with extraordinary powers that had mana and were tapu. Many were atua that had taken the material form of a tree, a log, a rock or a pond. Travellers treated these sacred landmarks with great respect as they would otherwise meet with disaster, or at the very least encounter stormy weather.

Often these tipua were of great antiquity and were located in especially significant places. Their presence there must have been reassuring to the people to whom they belonged, and a warning to others.

People passing a tipua tree or rock would often perform a ritual known as uruuru-whenua (or whakaū). They would place an offering of a green twig at its foot, and recite a ritual chant acknowledging the mana of the spirit within.

Despite the dictionary definitions, in most instances it is wrong to describe tipua (or tupua, a dialectal variant) as goblins or demons. Generally they were entities that possessed supernatural (more than normal, magic) powers, so were not what they seemed.

Tira-mākā
Companies of spirits

Crowds of spirits known as Tira-mākā could be seen at times travelling high up in the air, moving through space. Only the tohunga and other matakite [people with second sight] could see them. Ordinary people did not have this power.

Tira-mākā were sometimes thought to be wairua, souls of the dead, and sometimes to belong to a race of spirits which formerly inhabited these islands. The tohunga would perform rituals to disperse the spirits and prevent them from harming people.

Tītapu
Fine plumes

This name is associated with the plumes of the albatross, or sometimes those of the white heron or huia – these being the three most valued plumes worn in the hair by high-ranking people. The name might be given to the plume itself, or Tītapu might be regarded as the original owner of such plumes, or the place from which they could be obtained.

Toa-rangatira
Founder of Ngāti Toa

Toa-rangatira was born in south Kāwhia, perhaps in the later years of the seventeenth century. He was a younger son, and his father Korokino at first showed little interest in him. But Toa-rangatira was skilful and industrious, and bold and clever in outwitting his elder brother Koroau. Finally he won his father's approval and became his successor.

Toa-rangatira took part successfully in many battles. He lived a long life, and after his death his son, Marangai-paroa, became the leading rangatira in the region.

The people of Ngāti Toa trace their descent and take their name from Toa-rangatira. They remained in the Kāwhia district until 1821, then under the command of Te Rauparaha they set out on a long migration that took them eventually to Kapiti Island in the southern part of the North Island.

Tōhē
A southward journey

A renowned ancestor of Te Aupōuri, the people living furthest to the north, Tōhē belonged to the fourth generation of descendants from Pō, who arrived from Hawaiki on the *Kurahaupō*. Tōhē's daughter, Rānini-kura, married a rangatira who lived far to the south, and in his old age Tōhē determined to visit her.

Tōhē's relatives begged him not to go, but he set out boldly along the western shore with a single companion, a faithful servant named Ariki. Their way lay along the immense stretch of sand that was later named Te One Roa a Tōhē [Tōhē's long beach]. (Its English name is Ninety Mile Beach.)

As they went, Tōhē named the places they passed after events which occurred there. When, for instance, they came to a stream too deep to wade, Tōhē saw shoals of mullet in the water and he recited a chant asking for their assistance. Two very large mullet at once swam to the bank, the men rode across on their backs, and Tōhē named the stream Wai-kanae [Mullet stream].

They continued on, swam across Hokianga Harbour, then walked right down the coast to the high rocky outcrop of Maunganui (Maunganui Bluff). There they paused for a meal. But Tōhē now forgot that his atua, in taking him under their protection, had warned him never to look back. On a high point at Maunganui he wept for his home and he gazed back towards it. So he was abandoned by his guardian spirits and did not reach his daughter. He and his servant died there on Maunganui.

Tohunga
Guardians of sacred knowledge

In every section and sub-section of a people there were a number of tohunga [priests] of differing powers and status. At whatever level, the position of tohunga was generally hereditary, passing from father to son. Often the eldest son was chosen, but sometimes in a high-ranking family it would be a younger son. The father would secretly teach the boy, perhaps at night when others were asleep, or under a tree where no-one would disturb them. Much learning of ritual chants [karakia], sacred history and genealogies was required.

As well as passing on their knowledge and role within their own family, some famous tohunga taught at houses of learning [whare wānanga]. These schools were attended, generally in the winter months, by boys of high rank, who might travel considerable distances to do so.

An early writer, John White, tells us it was believed that 'one of the principal gods resides within a seer, and that there are many others who attend him in all his movements.' If any remarkable event took place, 'it was the business of the priest to expound its import. He was the guide of the people in almost all their concerns; in his hands was the direction of the policy of the tribe; nothing, in fact, save the ordinary actions, could be done without him . . . he was seer, physician, and general, also sorcerer, as well as priest.

'As priests, they had to conduct all ceremonies; as seers, by dreams and divinations they foretold the issue of events, and held conversation with the spiritual world, in songs taught them by spirits, shadowing forth the future . . . as wizards, by their incantations they bewitched those who might have given them or others offence; as physicians, they cured the sick by incantations; as generals, they led and determined the movements of war.'

A tohunga was highly tapu, and so by extension were his house, his possessions, everything he touched. Being tapu, he had to keep most carefully away from situations which could threaten his tapu and thereby insult his gods, who would vent their anger upon him. Uncontrolled contact with cooked food was especially destructive of tapu. After conducting an important ritual, a tohunga could sometimes eat and drink only when fed by an attendant.

Toi
An early inhabitant

There are many different myths about Toi, all related. In Arawa tradition, Toi-te-hua-tahi [Toi the only child] is a rangatira who stays behind in Hawaiki when *Te Arawa* sets out for Aotearoa. In a Ngāti Kahungunu story, Toi leaves Hawaiki to find his grandson, Whātonga, whose vessel has been swept out to sea; in the end Toi reaches Aotearoa and settles at Whakatāne, where Whātonga finds him.

But Toi is often the earliest ancestor living in this country, here before the waka arrive. In this role he is important especially to the peoples of the southern Bay of Plenty, the Urewera Mountains and the East Coast. Sometimes he is a descendant of Māui, who fished up the land then remained upon it. But usually it is simply said that he was the first man in this country.

His extended names include Toi-te-hua-tahi [Toi the only child] and Toi-kai-rākau [Toi who ate trees] – a name he gained, it is explained, because he did not possess the kūmara, so was dependant upon wild plant foods such as fernroot and the mamaku tree-fern. He is regarded as the source of these plants, having left them in the land as sustenance for his descendants. Sometimes it is said that he did not possess fire but ate his food raw. And some assert that he and his people never made war.

So Toi is often a transitional figure, one who lacks the normal human possessions of fire and the kūmara, and does not act as people do now.

This is not surprising, since his role in such traditions is to be the first person living in the land.

The name Toi must be a personification, like so many others. The word toi, in mystical contexts especially, refers to the origin and source of human beings, and to the earliest persons living in a land. His name, then, must mean something like Original-inhabitant.

Tokomaru
A west coast waka

The peoples of northern Taranaki, such as Te Āti Awa, Ngāti Mutunga and Ngāti Tama, often trace their origins to the *Tokomaru*, which brought their ancestors from the homeland of Hawaiki. In a song sung by Te Āti Awa, the men in charge of this waka are named as Tama-ariki and Rākeiora, and the vessel is said to have landed at the Mohakatino River. Ngāti Tama similarly regarded Tama-ariki as their founding ancestor and believed that Rākeiora, the tohunga on board the vessel, became after his death a god who protected the fertility of the kūmara.

Peoples tracing descent from the crew of *Tokomaru* spread north as far as the Mōkau River, which forms the boundary with the Tainui peoples. The southern boundary of the Tokomaru peoples, at Ōnukutaipari (south of New Plymouth), is shared with the Taranaki people, who claim descent from the *Kurahaupō*.

In a different tradition, not so widely known, the captain of the *Tokomaru* was Manaia. The vessel made landfall on the east coast, sailed around Muriwhenua (North Cape) and landed at the Tongaporutu River, where the crew left the god Rākeiora and their waka as well. Finally they settled at Waitara, having conquered the people they found there. They became, it is said, ancestors of Te Āti Awa.

In yet another tradition, *Tokomaru* is claimed by Ngāti Ruanui in southern Taranaki and by the Whanganui peoples. In these regions the vessel is captained by Rākeiora.

Tongameha
The spirit in control of eyes

It was believed that each part of the body was under the control of an atua. For the eyes, this spirit was Tongameha.

Tonganui
Owner of a house under the sea

Some peoples, such as Te Arawa and Ngā Puhi, say that when Māui was fishing for land, his fishhook caught the gableboard (some maintain, the doorway) of a house under the ocean which was owned by an old man named Tonganui. Māui slowly pulled up the house, and with it the fish on which people were to live.

In poetic metaphor, someone said to have fished up Tonganui is understood as having made an important 'catch' of some kind.

Tū
Origin of warfare

This fierce warrior is always an early ancestor, often one of the sons of the first parents, Rangi and Papa. In the best known version of the myth, from the Arawa peoples, the wind, Tāwhirimātea, attacks the earth, and only Tū is brave enough to withstand him. Afterwards Tū turns upon his other brothers, angry that they did not come to his assistance in the struggle with Tāwhirimātea. He kills these brothers, who are Tāne, Tangaroa, Rongo and Haumia (and who represent, respectively, birds and trees, fish, kūmara, and fernroot).

In this way Tū sets the pattern for the future. Because Tū attacked them in the beginning, human beings now, when they have performed the proper rituals, can safely kill and eat their relatives Tāne, Tangaroa, Rongo and Haumia, and they can cut down the trees, which are Tāne.

This episode also sets the pattern for warfare: men make war now because Tū did so in the beginning. When a baby boy was dedicated to a future life as a warrior, and again when rituals were performed over men about to go into battle, Tū was spoken of as the source and representative of the duty and honour they were accepting.

While it was mainly as a role model that he offered his assistance, offerings were made to him by those who were entering his realm. The body of the first enemy warrior killed was often offered to Tū.

Since Tū was primarily the originator of warfare in general, every people possessed as well a powerful god such as Kahukura, Uenuku or Maru, who was presented with offerings and asked for assistance in times of war.

Tūāhu
Sacred, ritual centres

Every settlement had at least one tūāhu, a shrine where the tohunga performed rituals of many kinds. It was the main site where atua were approached and offerings made to them.

The word tūāhu derives from a term, ahu, which refers to a heap or mound, and most tūāhu consisted essentially of such a mound. Often the mound was of earth, either a natural feature or, it seems, one specially constructed. Sometimes there were stones, which apparently might replace the hillock; a tohunga might select a place where there was a naturally occurring rock, or pile up a heap of unworked stones, or set one or more such stones upright in the ground. Occasionally a wooden pillar was employed.

Tūāhu seem to have varied considerably in form and location, even within a single region. Often they were at some distance from a settlement, hidden among tapu trees or flax bushes in a 'sacred place' [wāhi tapu] where the dead were laid to rest – and which served also as a repository for discarded garments and baskets of leftover food which had belonged to tohunga and other high-ranking people and were now too dangerously tapu to be left anywhere else.

Many communities must have had more than one tūāhu, since there are accounts of several kinds used for different purposes. In an emergency a tūāhu could be improvised; a tohunga could even cup his hand and use this as his shrine. But long-established tūāhu had great mana, and continuity was very important. When a tūāhu was to be moved, earth from the old site was taken to the new one.

Several tūāhu with extraordinary powers were established by the first ancestors to make the voyage from Hawaiki.

Tūheitia
A Waikato ancestor

In the sixteenth century this man was the leading rangatira in the lands to the south of the mouth of the Waikato River. After his death he became a taniwha.

His wife was Te Ata, sister of a man named Tahinga. When the two brothers-in-law went fishing one day, Tahinga became angry when Tūheitia caught many fish and he got none. He pretended the anchor stone was caught on the bottom and persuaded Tūheitia to dive for it, then as soon as Tūheitia was in the water he cut the anchor rope and paddled off.

In vain Tūheitia called to his brother-in-law; Tahinga only mocked him. And so Tūheitia sank down into the ocean and died.

Meanwhile Tūheitia's wife, Te Ata, was waiting. On Tahinga's return he pretended that Tūheitia was down by the shore, but Te Ata could not find him there. Then as she gazed out to sea, Tūheitia's arm thrust up through the ocean as a sign that he had become a taniwha. The arm was far out over the water, but the woman recognised it by a tattoo it bore. She knew then that her husband was dead.

Te Ata was pregnant at this time, and she later gave birth to a son, Māhanga, who became the founder of Ngāti Māhanga.

This is the story as told by Wiremu Te Whēoro; other authorities say that Tūheitia was killed by a visiting rangatira, Kōkako. Others again tell a similar story of Te Atai-o-rongo, saying that he married Rangi-waea of Te Ākau, was killed by his brother-in-law Hoeta, and became a taniwha. Afterwards his hand came as a sign to his wife in the house at night, and his wairua told her what she must do. When the hand returned, going out by the ridgepole, seawater dripped into the house.

His wife later had his son, Kaihu, who in time avenged his murder.

Tuhirangi
A taniwha guardian

This taniwha guided and protected Kupe's ship during his voyage from Hawaiki. Afterwards he was placed by Kupe in Raukawa (Cook Strait), in the dangerous waters at Te Au-miti (French Pass), a narrow passage with seething currents which separates Rangitoto (D'Urville Island) from the mainland of the South Island. There he welcomes and protects the crews of waka venturing into the region.

In the late nineteenth century, Tuhirangi became associated with a dolphin that was famous at the time. For more than twenty years, from 1888 onwards, a white dolphin inhabited a stretch of water off Pelorus Sound, north of French Pass. He regularly met and accompanied passing ships, and people formed such an attachment to the creature that the government gave him legal protection. While Pākehā called him Pelorus Jack, Māori people naturally recognised him as Tuhirangi.

Tūhoe-pōtiki
Founding ancestor of Tūhoe

The Tūhoe people of the Urewera Mountains acknowledge two main lines of descent, one indigenous and the other stemming from people who arrived from Hawaiki on *Mātaatua* and settled in the Whakatāne region. Of their Mātaatua ancestors the most important is Tūhoe-pōtiki, from whom they take their name.

Tūhoe-pōtiki was a grandson of Wairaka, who was a daughter of Tōroa, captain of the *Mātaatua*. As well he was descended from the local people, because the ship's crew had formed alliances through marriage with the peoples already in the region.

He should not be confused with Pōtiki, an indigenous ancestor of the Tūhoe people who lived much earlier and was the son Te Maunga [The mountain] and Hine-pūkohu-rangi [Sky-mist-woman]. This man Pōtiki had descendants who became known as Ngā Pōtiki. Many generations later, Ngā Pōtiki and another indigenous people, Te Tini o Toi [Toi's multitude], intermarried with the Mātaatua immigrants and produced the Tūhoe people.

Tū-horopunga
A menacing figure

In songs, sayings and myths, Tū-horopunga is a man who swallows things down. People spoke of him when talking about greed: 'Tū-horopunga is at his work again' was a comment on someone eating more than a fair share. Occasionally too he was thought to swallow human beings. A poet in the Far North spoke of someone who had died as having been swallowed by Tū-horopunga – so he could, with others, be blamed for death.

Tūhourangi
A very tall man

An early ancestor descended from people who arrived on *Te Arawa*, Tūhourangi was one of the eight children of Rangitihi. He had two sons, Uenuku-kōpako and Taketake-hiku-roa, and was founder of the Tūhourangi people (many of whom, until the eruption of 1886, lived by Lake Tarawera).

According to tradition Tūhourangi was enormously tall, some say about three metres in height. To promote the fertility of the kūmara crop, his bones were disinterred every spring and were placed beside the cultivations on Mokoia Island while the planting rituals were being performed.

Tūkete
A precursor

Some South Island writers that this man arrived there from Hawaiki before anyone else, when the seas were still very rough. To enable later voyagers to reach the country safely, he recited ritual chants to calm the waves.

When he came ashore he found that the land was tapu and inhabited by fairies [tūrehu], and that it was still soft and shaking. To prepare it for human habitation, he destroyed the tapu and dispelled the fairies by lighting ritual ovens.

Another man named Tūkete, a rangatira of Ngāti Māmoe, is said to have possessed a taniwha guardian (see the next entry). His taniwha may originally have been associated with this earlier, mythical explorer.

Tūkete's guardian
A taniwha down south

A taniwha in the form of a great shark, as long as a house and spotted red and black, used to inhabit the Raggedy Passage, a channel between Codfish and Stewart Islands (as they are now known). This taniwha was at first the guardian of Tūkete, a Ngāti Māmoe rangatira who lived nearby. When Tūkete was killed in battle, the taniwha continued to haunt the coast where his master had lived and died.

Tumutumu-whenua
An ancestor from the ground

The people of Ngāti Whātua lived originally in the North Cape region. Later they moved to the Kaitaia and Hokianga districts, then further south to Kaipara and Tāmaki.

They believed that their first ancestor, Tumutumu-whenua, was not of this world but came up from the ground. However his wife, Repo, did belong to this world, because her people were the fairies [patupaiarehe].

Tuna
The phallic eel

The word tuna is the ordinary term for an eel, and Tuna is the personification of the eel. In South Island tradition, Tuna came down from the sky because the upper regions were too dry. Another belief, there and elsewhere, was that he was killed for having seduced Māui's wife Hina (or Hine) while she was bathing. Māui revenged himself by digging a trench (and also, it is sometimes said, placing ten skids inside it). When Tuna made his way along this watercourse he was chopped to bits by Māui.

This episode is reminiscent of one of the many ways of catching eels. In some places such as Wairewa (Lake Forsyth), where a shingle bank separates a lake from the ocean, trenches are cut towards the sea and the eels are trapped within them.

When Tuna was chopped up by Māui, the pieces turned into other life forms. Tuna's head went to the rivers and became freshwater eels, his tail reached the ocean and became the conger eel, the long hair-like nostrils on the tip of his upper jaw turned into vines and certain other plants, and his blood coloured the rimu, the tōtara and other trees that now have reddish wood.

Tū-nui-o-te-ika
A powerful atua

In several regions Tū-nui-o-te-ika was a powerful war god. Among Ngāti Kahungunu on the East Coast, he was believed to have come from Hawaiki in the *Tākitimu;* some said he led the way as a ball of fire. His appearance as a comet foretokened disaster.

Tuoro
Giant eels

These monsters live in swamps and lakes and occasionally come up out of the water to feed on plants by the shore. A tuoro will chase and kill anyone it sees, unless the person is able to escape by setting fire to the vegetation (because the eel cannot pass over ground that has been burnt). Tuoro have large lumps on their tails with which they kill their victims. They howl like dogs, and can make their way underground.

Tuputupu-whenua
An ancestor beneath

In the Far North, the people of Ngā Puhi at Hokianga believed that Tuputupu-whenua [Sprung from the ground] was an early ancestor who now lived under the ground with his wife, Kūī. These two were the original inhabitants of the country.

The navigator Kupe came from Hawaiki in search of Tuputupu-whenua and found him at last in Hokianga. On his return Kupe spoke to Nuku-tawhiti, who had decided to sail to Aotearoa, and told him where he would find Tuputupu-whenua. But when Nuku, on the *Māmari*, reached the mouth of the Hokianga Harbour, Tuputupu-whenua went down into the ground and there remained.

Tura
Originator of childbirth

In some versions of this myth, Tura sets out on a voyage with the evil Whiro then discovers that their waka is going down to death. When they pass an island (sometimes it is Hawaiki), Tura leaves the vessel and Whiro continues on without him.

Tura lives on the island with the people he finds there, who are Nukumaitore's Descendants; in some versions they are all women, in others there are men as well. These people are not fully human and they make no use of fire. Tura teaches them how to kindle fire, and they are delighted with the food he cooks.

The people give him a wife, then when she is pregnant they come to cut her open and remove the child, because that is the only way they know. Tura chases them away and erects a pole for his wife to press on during childbirth; he recites a ritual chant to ease the birth, and the child is born. So then the people see that there is a pathway along which a child should go.

Tura continues to live there, but one day his wife sees grey hairs on his head and discovers that he will grow old and die. Afterwards Tura becomes homesick and longs for his former wife and his son. He sets out to find them, and on the way he becomes ill. His son learns of this in a dream, comes seeking him, and cares for him until he recovers.

Tūrongo and Māhina-ā-rangi
An important marriage

Tūrongo grew up at Te Whaanga, just north of the Aotea Harbour, perhaps in the early sixteenth century. He was of distinguished descent, being a son of Tāwhao, a leading rangatira, and Tāwhao's principal wife. Yet his circumstances were difficult, because Tāwhao's secondary wife had given birth to a son shortly before he was born. Since this boy, Whatihua, was the elder of the two brothers, he was regarded as superior in rank despite his mother's inferior status. Inevitably these men grew up as rivals.

In this situation Tūrongo's marriage was crucial. At first it seemed he would marry Ruapūtahanga, a high-ranking woman of Ngāti Ruanui in southern Taranaki, but Whatihua cunningly put an end to this arrangement and took the woman for himself.

Tūrongo in his grief abandoned his home and set out on a long journey to Heretaunga (Hawke's Bay). There at Kahotea he stayed with a rangatira, Angiangi; he fell in love with Angiangi's beautiful daughter Māhina-ā-rangi, and she returned his love. Angiangi willingly accepted Tūrongo as a son-in-law, and the two were married. After a time Tūrongo returned to prepare a home for Māhina-a-rangi.

At this point Tāwhao wisely called his two sons together and divided his lands between them. Tūrongo moved inland and built a pā on a hill, Rangiātea, in the central basin of the Waipā River, and Māhina-ā-rangi soon arrived with their newborn son, Raukawa.

Many peoples trace their origin to Raukawa and his descendants, and Tūrongo's marriage with Māhina-ā-rangi provides an important link between the Tainui peoples and those of the East Coast.

Tūtaeporoporo
Revenge for a master's death

In the Rangitīkei district a couple of generations after the arrival of the *Aotea*, a man named Tūariki made a pet of a young shark he had caught. The creature grew big, and soon became a taniwha the size of a whale. His name was Tūtaeporoporo.

Some time later, warriors from Whanganui visited Rangitīkei and killed Tūariki, then took his body back home and cooked it. When Tūtaeporoporo went in search of his master, the scent from the oven reached him on the wind.

So the taniwha swam up the Whanganui River to revenge his master's death. He made his home in a pool beneath a high ridge, Taumaha-aute (now known also as Shakespeare Cliff), and he attacked and devoured men and women travelling up and down the river.

When people in the region realised what was happening they left their homes and fled inland. Then a man named Tama-āhua visited Waitōtara to ask Aokehu, a famous killer of taniwha, if he would help them. Aokehu agreed to do so, and next day he and his men reached the Whanganui.

Upriver from the taniwha's home, this brave warrior told the people to make a wooden chest with a close-fitting lid. When this was done, he entered the chest and instructed them to fasten the lid and set him afloat.

As Aokehu approached the taniwha's lair, Tūtaeporoporo smelt the good smell of food, rushed out and swallowed the chest. Then Aokehu, inside the monster, began to recite ritual chants, one to put him to sleep and another to make him float to the surface. The chants did their work and the now helpless taniwha drifted ashore. He was killed at once and the lashings were cut from Aokehu's chest.

Inside the creature they found the bodies of men, women and children. These they buried in their pā. Tūtaeporopo was left as food for the birds of the air and the fish of the sea, and the people returned rejoicing to their homes.

Tū-tāmure
An ugly warrior

Tū-tāmure, a great-grandson of the famous Tamatea, spent his youth at Ōpōtiki. When he became a man, he and his elder brother, Taipūnoa, set out on an expedition of war. At Te Māhia (Māhia Peninsula) their men lay siege to the Maunga-a-kahia Pā.

Tū-tāmure did not know the pā was under the command of Kahungunu, a relative of his who was now an old man. Nor did Kahungunu know the identity of the formidable young rangatira who was leading the attack upon his people. So Kahungunu sent a man to call from the palisades and ask for this information, and Tū-tāmure himself, in proud metaphorical language, divulged his name. Kahungunu realised then that Tū-tāmure was a relative, and to make peace he asked his daughter, Tauhei-kurī, to go out of the pā and marry him.

Tauhei-kurī went and sat beside Tū-tāmure, but when he made overtures to her that night she would have nothing to do with him. In the morning it rained, and Tū-tāmure saw his reflection in a pool of water. He looked closely, and saw that he was ugly. He said, 'Was it for nothing that this woman wouldn't have me? No, it's because I'm really ugly.'

As for the woman, she married his brother Taipūnoa instead. The people in the pā were saved, and the war party returned to their own homes.

Tū-tangata-kino
A reptile, or a taniwha

In some parts of the west coast of the North Island, this atua, whose name means Tū-the-evil-man, took the form of an especially powerful reptile. It was thought that spirits in the form of reptiles could crawl through people's mouths while they were asleep and gnaw their stomachs, producing illness, and Tū-tangata-kino was sometimes the reptile held responsible for this.

But such powers worked both ways. Because he was so dangerous, Tū-tangata-kino was a highly effective guardian when the proper ceremonies were performed. A man about to go on a journey might ensure his wife's faithfulness by reciting a chant naming Tū-tangata-kino, with Maru, as the guardians of her virtue in his absence.

On the Whanganui River a different story is told. In this tradition, Tū-tangata-kino is a taniwha who guided the *Aotea* during its voyage from Hawaiki and afterwards settled at Pātea with its captain, Turi.

Tūtara-kauika
A guardian taniwha

Tūtara-kauika is an ocean taniwha, in the form of a whale, who protects the people with whom he is associated. In one tradition he accompanied the *Tākitimu* to Aotearoa, then remained in the sea by Wairoa as the guardian of his people. He sometimes saves people in danger of drowning, and may then be accompanied by a taniwha named Te Wehenga-kauika. Occasionally he leads a group of such taniwha, all in the form of whales.

Tūtaua
A singing log

When Haumapūhia created Lake Waikaremoana in the Urewera Mountains, she placed upon its waters a tōtara log known as Tūtaua. For many generations this log drifted around the lake, singing in an eerie whistling voice. He was a taniwha, and was also spoken of as a tipua – an entity with an uncanny life of its own.

Tū-tawake
A fierce warrior

Sometimes Tū-tawake is an extended name for Tū, who initiated warfare. In other traditions, Tū (or Tū-mata-uenga) is the primary figure and comes very early in the genealogies, while Tū-tawake comes later and has a separate existence as a warrior. This is the case in some parts of the East Coast and in the South Island, where Tū-tawake is the son of an evil woman named Houmea.

Tūtekohe
A rangatira and his dog

When this high-ranking man in the Tūranga (Gisborne) district was entertaining visitors, he would allow his dog to lick the fat from the tops of the containers of preserved birds which stood ready for his guests. He was so powerful that his visitors were forced to ignore this insult.

Then when a rangatira named Rākaipākā visited Tūtekohe's pā with some companions, Tūtekohe did worse than this. The two rangatira were apparently far from friendly. The story is that Tūtekohe's potted birds were presented to his dog rather than his guest. Rākaipākā received only the bones the dog did not eat.

Rākaipākā went home showing no signs of anger, but that night someone came to Tūtekohe's pā and lured his dog outside. The creature was killed, taken away and eaten.

Tūtekohe knew next morning what had happened. His warriors attacked Rākaipākā's people and drove them south to the Māhia Peninsula and Nūhaka – where their descendants, Ngāti Rākaipākā, still live today.

Tū-te-koropanga
Originator of plant obstructions

Tū-te-koropanga's main obstructions are prickly plants. They represent insuperable obstacles, or sometimes obstacles which can be overcome only with great difficulty, and for this reason they were spoken of by poets and orators.

Tū-te-nganahau
The source of trouble

On the west coast of the North Island, the fierce Tū-te-nganahau is sometimes a son of the first parents, Rangi and Papa; it is he who cuts the sinews that join these two in the beginning. Tū-te-nganahau seems here to be an extended name for Tū, who in most parts of the country initiates strife and the practice of warfare.

Sometimes, however, Tū-te-nganahau is a figure with a separate existence who may act in association with Tū (or Tū-matauenga).

Tutumaiao
Spirits on the beaches

If you are walking along a beach and see, far ahead, misty forms like people which retreat as you advance, these are the Tutumaiao. Some say they visit the beaches from their homes in the sea.

Tū-whakairi-ora
A great warrior

In the mid-sixteenth century a rangatira named Poroumātā was killed at Whareponga by the people of Ngāti Ruanuku among whom he had been living. Most of his relatives chose to ignore this but his daughter, Te Ataākura, planned her revenge. To raise a son to avenge the murder, she married Ngātihau of Ūawa (Tolaga Bay). She and her husband then went to live at Ōpōtiki, where he had relatives. Their first child was a girl and she wept for her hopes. But the second was a boy, Tū-whakairi-ora.

As he grew up, Tū-whakairi-ora was constantly reminded that he would avenge his grandfather. Strengthening rituals were performed and he was carefully trained. When he had won fame as a warrior, he set out to achieve his destiny.

From Ōpōtiki he made his way around the coast to the mouth of the Wharekāhika River (at Hicks Bay), where his relative Te Aotaki was the leading rangatira. Te Aotaki received him with honour and gave him his daughter, Ruataupare, as his wife.

For some years Tū-whakairi-ora lived with Ruataupare on land given her as a marriage settlement, then when he was sufficiently established in the region he summoned allies from his wife's people and his own relatives at Ōpōtiki. He led an army to Whareponga, the home of Ngāti Ruanuku, and there gained a great victory, avenging the death of his grandfather.

Afterwards he continued to live at Wharekāhika. His descendants, who are known as Te Whānau-a-Tū-whakairi-ora, became one of the strongest sections of Ngāti Porou.

Ruataupare eventually quarrelled with Tū-whakairi-ora and set out with her followers to found a people of her own. She conquered Te Wahine-iti, an ancient people at Tokomaru Bay, and her descendants, Te Whānau-a-Ruataupare, are living there still.

Tū-whakararo
A murdered relative

The warrior Whakatau is one of the main avengers in Māori tradition. The man whose death he avenges is usually Tū-whakararo, an elder brother (or sometimes father) who has been murdered by people living in a great house known as Te Tihi-o-Manōno.

In some versions of the myth, Tū-whakararo dies while visiting a brother-in-law. In others he visits his mother's brothers and the trouble begins when he falls in love with a high-ranking woman, Maurea, and she returns his love. Another suitor challenges Tū-whakararo to a wrestling match. Tū-whakararo twice defeats this jealous rival, then goes to put on his cloak. Having been unable to beat him in a fair fight, the rival seizes this opportunity; he blinds him by throwing sand in his eyes, then kills him.

Tūwharetoa
Founder of Ngāti Tūwharetoa

This powerful rangatira lived at Kawerau in the sixteenth century. His mother, Haahuru, belonged to the earliest peoples in the region, those descended from Toi, Te Hapū-oneone and Kawerau, while his father, Mawake-taupō, belonged to the Arawa and Mātaatua peoples and was a seventh-generation descendant of the great tohunga Ngātoro-i-rangi. Tūwharetoa therefore obtained his right to land from his mother's ancestors and his mana from his father's ancestors.

A wise leader, valiant warrior and expert carver, Tūwharetoa had several wives and many children. His descendants later conquered Ngāti Hotu, an early people in possession of the Taupō region.

Uenuku
A great rangatira in Hawaiki

Uenuku, in many myths, is a great man who lives in Hawaiki and is always triumphant when he engages in battle. In the traditions of both *Te Arawa* and the *Aotea*, people threatened by Uenuku are forced to migrate from Hawaiki. Māia, in an East Coast myth, comes for the same reason, and so do Ruawhārō and Tūpai on the *Tākitimu*, although they manage to revenge themselves first. In yet another East Coast myth, Uenuku is indirectly responsible for Paikea's journey from Hawaiki on the back of a whale.

In stories such as these, Uenuku is a man rather than a god. Some peoples, however, know Uenuku as a powerful atua who protected his people and was appealed to in times of war. This is, for example, his significance for the Tainui peoples.

Uenuku-tuwhatu
A life-giving rock

This man, the elder son of Whatihua and Ruapūtahanga, lived at Kāwhia and Taranaki in the sixteenth century. At the end of his human existence he turned to stone and he is now a sacred rock, a tipua standing near the mouth of a stream in the Kāwhia Harbour. In this form he was believed to possess the power of making childless women conceive, and many women visited him for this reason.

Ureia
A taniwha at Hauraki

Ureia, a quiet creature who resembled a whale, was the taniwha guardian of the people of Ngāti Tamaterā at Hauraki. One day he was visited by Haumia, the taniwha guardian of another people who were living by the Manukau Harbour. Haumia stayed a while, then invited Ureia to pay a return visit to the Manukau. Ureia agreed and the two set off.

But this was a plot. Haumia had promised his tohunga to lure Ureia to the Manukau, and men were waiting to kill him. According to one story, Ureia was caught in a baited trap; others say that Haumia led Ureia into a snare that had been placed at the entrance to the harbour, and that Ureia fought for four low tides and four high tides before he died.

His death led to a war between the two peoples.

Uru and Ngangana
Ancient names

In different traditions these names are differently associated. On the East Coast, the two names (or closely similar ones) appear in genealogies as early ancestors. In Taranaki songs, Uru and Ngangana are usually the owners of two waka, the *Rangi-totohu* and the *Rangi-kekero*, which convey people to death and destruction. In Ngāti Kahungunu traditions concerning the high god Io, an atua named Uru-te-ngangana is the first-born of the seventy sons of Rangi and Papa; because of his high rank he is angry when a younger son, Tāne, presumes to separate their parents.

In such traditions the menacing nature of this figure (or figures) probably follows from the fact that the word ngangana can mean 'rage, bluster, make a disturbance'.

Uruao
A southern waka

This vessel set out for Aotearoa from distant islands, captained by Rākaihautū. It made landfall in the northernmost part of the North Island but the crew, finding this island inhabited, sailed down the west coast, crossed to the South Island and landed at Whakatū (Nelson). No one was living in the south. Rākaihautū was the first man to light a fire there.

The *Uruao* brought to the south the ancestors of the Waitaha people, also (some say) two kinds of beings with extraordinary powers, Te Kāhui Tipua and Te Rapuwai. These beings now found places to live.

Meanwhile the humans divided into two groups and set out to explore the land. Rākaihautū led a party through the interior, taking with him his digging stick, and thinking that the country needed lakes he dug them out at intervals. His son Te Rakihouia (or Te Rokohouia) sailed along the east coast with the other group, investigating the rich sea-food resources in the region.

Rākaihautū and his son met in the far south, then Rākaihautū and his men walked back along the coast; the last of the lakes he dug were Waihora (Lake Ellesmere) and Wairewa (Lake Forsyth). He then settled at nearby Akaroa.

Most of the lakes believed to have been dug out by Rākaihautū were in fact created by glaciers. Since they had clearly been excavated by some agency it was quite logical to think they had been dug by the first man to arrive from Hawaiki.

Rākaihautū is sometimes known as Rākaihaitū.

Waihuka and Tū-te-amoamo
A murderous brother

Two brothers once lived alone together; the younger was Waihuka and the elder Tū-te-amoamo. Then Waihuka married a beautiful woman, Hine-i-te-kakara [Sweet scented woman], and Tū-te-amoamo wanted her for himself. So he asked his brother to go fishing, and Waihuka agreed.

When their waka was full of fish, Tū-te-amoamo called, 'Pull up the anchor.'

Waihuka said, 'It's stuck, I can't manage it.'

His elder brother insisted he must dive to free it, and Waihuka dived down. At once Tū-te-amoamo cut the rope and hoisted the sail, leaving him there to die.

So the younger brother floated about in the water, wondering how he could save himself. He called, 'Albatross, carry me to land!'

But the albatross paid no attention.

He called like this to all the birds then all the fish, but none of them listened. Then the whale, his ancestor, heard his call and took him to the land.

Meanwhile Tū-te-amoamo had gone ashore. When Hine-i-te-kakara saw him, she thought her husband must be dead. She went into her house and wept for him.

That evening Tū-te-amoamo came and called to her, but she would not answer. Inside she was digging a hole by the wall, and she at last escaped and went along the beach looking for her husband's body. The whale told her where to go, and she found Waihuka alive. They wept together, then planned their revenge.

That evening Tū-te-amoamo came to the house again and called to his brother's wife, 'Hine-i-te-kakara, open the door!'

Hine-i-te-kakara said, 'Yes, come in, Tū-te-amoamo.'

The moment he entered, Waihuka leapt forward with his taiaha and struck his head from his shoulders.

This occurred at Marokopa, near Kāwhia. Hine-i-te-kakara and Waihuka had many children, who became renowned warriors and ancestors of Ngāti Apakura.

Wairaka
The woman who acted like a man

When *Mātaatua* landed at a river mouth after its voyage from Hawaiki, the men on board neglected their vessel, securing only its stern. Then they went off to climb a hill and view their new land.

Next morning the waves were breaking over *Mātaatua*. The captain's daughter Wairaka, realising what was happening, called, 'The ship will be broken!'

But the men did not listen. They were distracted by the discoveries they were making.

So Wairaka called, 'Oh, I must turn myself into a man!'

She said this to shame the men, and she succeeded – though some say she still had to secure *Mātaatua* herself. Her words were remembered, and the name Whakatāne [Turn into a man] was given to the region and its river in memory of this occurrence (though there are some who claim it was her aunt, Muriwai, who did this).

Later, a party of travellers from Tāmaki (the Auckland region) came to Whakatāne. Wairaka fell in love with one of them, a handsome man who was a fine dancer, and she made up her mind to marry him. When everyone was asleep, she went over to the place in the house where he had been lying. And to show he was her lover, she scratched his face before she left him.

Next morning she told her father what had happened and sent him to fetch the man whose face she had scratched. Then she found she had been deceived. Someone else among the visitors, an ugly man named Mai, had noticed her interest and managed to change places with the man she loved. It was Mai who bore the scratch, and Mai whom she now married.

Her horrified exclamation became a saying: 'Oh what could I do, in the darkness that confused Wairaka?' [Ā, me aha koa e au, i te pō i raru ai Wairaka?]

Wairua
The soul that travels

Within a person there were believed to be two presences, a wairua and a hau, which can be termed souls. Both were implanted at conception by the father. The hau, which was associated with the breath, remained with the body until death, then disappeared. The other soul, the wairua, left the body during sleep and travelled around.

This belief explained the experience of sleep and of dreaming. If someone dreamt of a distant place, their wairua was visiting that place. If they dreamt of a person, their wairua was greeting that person's wairua. If they dreamt of the dead, their wairua had visited the underworld. During their travels the wairua were watchful and would convey a warning if necessary.

While the hau disappeared at death, the wairua continued to exist and three days later it set out for the underworld, home of the dead. It might, however, come back to visit living relatives, often to warn of impending danger.

Waiwaia
A taniwha of Ngāti Maniapoto

Waiwaia was once a tapu tōtara tree on the slopes of the Rangitoto Range, near the headwaters of the Waipā River. An old tohunga used to sit beneath it, but his atua became angry and sent the tree down into the earth and the water. The tree became a taniwha, and now goes drifting along the Waipā and the lower Waikato. It goes floating along, then strands itself in a place; if it is recognised, it will soon leave for somewhere else. It keeps visiting places like this, lying there for a while then moving on.

There is a saying, 'The many stranding-places of Waiwaia' [Ko rau paenga o Waiwaia]. If someone in a party of travellers asked where they would spend the night, another might reply, 'Oh, at the many stranding-places of Waiwaia.'

Wehi-nui-a-mamao
Source of the stars

In Heretaunga (Hawke's Bay) and the South Island, Wehi-nui-a-mamao is the man from whom the stars were acquired in the beginning. After Tāne had created the world by pushing Rangi the sky upwards, he wanted to make his father beautiful. He acquired the stars from Wehi-nui-a-mamao, he threw them up, and Rangi shone brightly.

Wehi-nui-a-mamao's stars are sometimes said to be the fastenings, the toggles, on his four dogskin cloaks – these being apparently equivalent to the expanse of the sky.

Whaitiri
A powerful woman in the sky

The name Whaitiri means Thunder. This woman lived in the sky, and was a cannibal; when she heard about a man down below called Kai-tangata she visited him, thinking his name must mean Eat-people. Soon she married him, but afterwards she waited in vain to be offered a meal of human flesh. Kai-tangata was not a cannibal but a peaceful fisherman.

Presently Whaitiri and Kai-tangata had a son, Hemā. By this time she had become tired of waiting for human meat. In her anger she recited a ritual chant to make the fish swim away, and Kai-tangata caught nothing when he went out each day.

Then Whaitiri made up her mind to return to the sky. She recited a chant to make fish plentiful once more, then a cloud came down and took her up.

In time Hemā had two sons, Tāwhaki and Karihi. When they grew up, these young men determined to visit their grandmother. Karihi failed in this difficult undertaking but Tāwhaki succeeded, and found Whaitiri at her home. She was blind, and was sitting counting out ten taro for her grand-daughters. Tāwhaki stole her taro one by one, then he healed her eyes and she could see. Afterwards she helped Tāwhaki to win one of her grand-daughters as his wife.

This is the story told by Ngāti Porou on the East Coast. Elsewhere there are differences. On the west coast of the North Island, Whaitiri had an especially important position. In one early account she is the first old goddess of the ages of darkness [te atua kuia tuatahi o ngā pō], and it is she (rather than Tāne) who recites the chant that leads to the separation of the earth and sky.

In west coast tradition, Whaitiri married Kai-tangata and had three sons. When Kai-tangata complained that the children were dirty, Whaitiri was offended and went back to the sky, but first she built for Kai-tangata the first heketua [latrine]. This was an event of consequence, because these structures had ritual significance. Whaitiri's heketua is still to be seen amongst the stars.

On the west coast as elsewhere, Hemā's son Tāwhaki succeeds in climbing to the sky. He encounters Whaitiri there and restores her sight.

Her residence in the sky, her association with thunder, and her control over fertility in the form of both food and grand-daughters make Whaitiri a highly tapu and powerful figure. It is not surprising that while she could be dangerous, even demonic, she was a most prestigious ancestor.

Whakaahu
Star of spring growth

Whakaahu is a star that brings the spring, the time when plants and foods of all kinds are stimulated to growth (this being the meaning of the word whakaahu). It rises at dawn in early August and is probably Castor, though some have thought it may be Pollux.

Whakaotirangi
A far-sighted woman

In the traditions of both the *Tainui* and *Te Arawa*, Whakaotirangi is the wife of the man who captains the ship on its voyage from Hawaiki. In each case she is responsible for ensuring that the kūmara arrives safely in Aotearoa.

According to the Tainui story, Whakaotirangi was the senior wife of Hoturoa. When the rest of the crew ate their seed kūmara on the way, she prudently kept hers tied up in a corner of her basket. Afterwards she planted them in soil brought from the homeland, and they flourished exceedingly.

The Arawa peoples, on the other hand, say that Whakaotirangi was the wife of Tama-te-kapua (who had stolen her from Ruaeo). When Ngātoro-i-rangi sent the vessel down towards Te Parata, the monster at the edge of the sky, most of the crew lost their seed kūmara but Whakaotirangi saved some in a tightly fastened corner of her basket. Later she planted them and they grew prolifically.

Whakatau
The warrior who gains revenge

It was the sacred duty of a warrior to avenge the killing of a relative. One of the most important of the avenging warriors in Māori tradition is Whakatau.

He is very small, and a youngest son; sometimes he is known as Whakatau-pōtiki [Whakatau the youngest]. All his brothers are tall, yet he is the one chosen to revenge the death of Tū-whakararo. With a few carefully chosen companions he sets out to do this.

In one version of the myth, from Ngāti Ruanui in southern Taranaki, when Whakatau enters the house of his enemies the bones of the murdered Tū-whakararo cry and wail in recognition. Whakatau runs from the house and jumps on the roof, throws a noose down through the smoke-hole, and catches one then another of the enemy warriors. Lastly he sets fire to the house. It burns to the ground with the people inside.

There are numerous variations, though Whakatau's main deed is always much the same. Usually he avenges the death of Tū-whakararo, his father (or elder brother), and it is Apakura, his mother (or occasionally sister) who asks him to undertake this task. Usually the enemy, who live over the sea, are the people of Te Āti Hāpai, and their leading man is Poporokewa. Their great house is Te Tihi-o-Manōno, or Te Uru-o-Manōno.

Whakaue
A Rotorua ancestor

The western shores of Lake Rotorua, and Mokoia Island as well, are the traditional territory of Ngāti Whakaue. These people take their name from Whakaue-kaipapa, son of Uenuku-kōpako.

With his principal wife, Rangiuru, Whakaue had six children. The three eldest sons were Tawakeheimoa, Ngārara-nui and Tuteaiti, the younger sons were Tūtānekai and Kōpako, and their daughter, the youngest, was Tupaharanui. The famous Tūtānekai was a stepson, being the son of Rangiuru and a visiting rangatira, Tūwharetoa.

Whānau-moana
A winged man

On the west coast of the North Island, Whānau-moana [Born of the sea] was the progenitor of a winged race of human beings. He owed his name to his miraculous birth, which occurred after Turi, captain of the *Aotea*, arrived from Hawaiki. When Turi's third son was born the afterbirth was thrown into the sea, then later it was washed up on the shore and found to be alive. Some people cared for the winged boy who grew from it, and he became a man.

Whāngai-mokopuna
Origin of the Manawatū Gorge

This taniwha used to live at Motuiti (near the present town of Foxton). He was the pet of the Rangitāne people there, who used to bring him basketfuls of eels, but one day some children gave him only the heads of eels. Infuriated, Whāngai-mokopuna ate one of the children instead, then fled from the child's relatives.

He swam up the Manawatū River, then at its junction with the Tāmaki River he avoided a long detour by cutting straight through the hills, forming the Manawatū Gorge. Afterwards he made his home in the headwaters of the Mangapuaka Stream, another of the Manawatū's many tributaries.

Whānui
The harvest star

Whānui is Vega, fifth brightest of the visible stars. He was regarded as the father of the kūmara; when he appeared before dawn in late February he was thought to be coming from Hawaiki, and his presence was a sign that the kūmara crop had matured and could soon be harvested.

Whānui's younger brother, Rongo-māui, once visited him in the sky, wanting to obtain the kūmara for human beings. When Whānui refused his request he stole the kūmara and brought it down, and ever since this time the kūmara has been cultivated upon the earth.

Whare-matangi

A search for a father

A man named Ngarue left his wife and moved south from Kāwhia to Waitara. Since his wife was pregnant at the time, he gave her a magic dart [teka tipua] which would enable their son, when he grew up, to find his father. (Darts of this kind were light rods about a metre in length.)

The boy was born, and was named Whare-matangi. When he became a man he followed his father's instructions; with his mother's assistance he cast the dart, reciting a chant, and it flew far away. He found it and threw once more; this time a rainbow showed where it lay. Again he threw, and again, then on the fifth throw the dart landed on the marae of the house where Ngarue was living. His father recognised him as his son, and performed over him the tohi ritual that dedicated him to his future life.

Whātonga

Toi's grandson

An early ancestor named Toi occurs in the genealogies of many different peoples. Sometimes this man lives in Aotearoa in the beginning, and sometimes his home is in Hawaiki. Often his son is Rauru and his grandson is Whātonga.

While there are many stories about Toi and some about Rauru, in most places little is said about Whātonga. He is, however, regarded as the founding ancestor of the Rangitāne people, in the region of the Manawatū River. The Rangitāne people regard Whātonga as a son of Rongoueroa, who lived some twenty-seven generations ago, and a grandson of Toi.

Their authorities say that Whātonga captained *Kurahaupō* on its voyage from Hawaiki, and that the other leading men on board were the navigator, Ruatea, and Popoto. They settled first at Nukutaurua, on the northern shore of Te Māhia (the Māhia Peninsula), where their waka became a reef.

Whātonga later moved south to what is now the Hastings district, settling among people already there. Ruatea apparently also went south, for his son (some say, grandson) Apa-hāpai-taketake became the founding ancestor of Ngāti Apa in the Rangitīkei district. Popoto, who seems to have remained at Te Māhia, became an ancestor of Ngāti Kahungunu.

There is a story that Whātonga's voyage to Aotearoa occurred after he captained a vessel that was blown out to sea during a race between waka in Hawaiki. His grief-stricken grandfather, Toi, sailed in search of him, while Whātonga meanwhile returned home safely. Whātonga then went looking for Toi, and in Aotearoa he found him at last at Whakatāne. Afterwards he sailed to Nukutaurua.

Whatu kura

Stones of great mana

Smooth, highly tapu pebbles known as whatu, or whatu kura, were important in Māori religion, being employed in many rituals. This word whatu means 'stone', not an ordinary stone but a special one employed in this way. The adjective kura means 'precious' and sometimes 'crimson'.

Whatu kura were often red or reddish, sometimes white. Usually they were a couple of centimetres, or less, in length. Articles employed in ritual were often small, since this distinguished them from the mass of ordinary, common objects.

As well, whatu were set apart by their sacred origins. They were believed to have been brought from Hawaiki by the tohunga on the ancestral waka, or to have been acquired by an early ancestor (Tāwhaki, or Tāne) from the heights of the sky.

Whiro

Source of evil

This man performed many evil deeds, introducing into the world such practices as murder, cannibalism, adultery, theft and lying. Because he established precedents for behaviour like this, he can be held responsible for the actions of those who have imitated him. As well he carries people off to death, so can be blamed for death.

In the best-known story, told on the East Coast and in other places, Whiro sets off, accompanied at first by Tura, on a sinister voyage that ends down below. His waka is the *Hotu-te-ihi*, or *Hotu-te-ihi-rangi* or *Whatu-te-ihi*.

On the west coast of the North Island, a different story was told (see the entries for Te Whare Kura and Monoa). But the myth of the waka's voyage was known as well in this region, although perhaps not in detail.

Another tradition, from Ngāti Kahungunu, has the evil Whiro jealous of his younger brother Tāne, and in conflict with him (see the entry for Io).

Whiro-nui
Captain of the *Nukutere*

There is apparently no detailed account of the voyage of the *Nukutere* from Hawaiki. We are told that among the crew were the captain, Whiro-nui, his wife Ārai-ara, and two tohunga, Mārere-o-tonga and Takataka-pū-tonga. The waka landed just south of East Cape and the people settled in that region.

Some years later, the early ancestor Paikea was making his way southward along the coast, having travelled from Hawaiki on the back of a whale. At Te Kautuku he met and married Huturangi, daughter of Whiro-nui and Ārai-ara.

A note on the language

In nearly all cases, Māori words do not change their form in the plural. This usage has been retained in the present work in the case of Māori words that have been adopted into New Zealand English. Macrons (for example, ā, ē) indicate long vowels. Square brackets enclose translations of names; parentheses enclose present-day place names.

Glossary

Terms which are also the subject of an encyclopedia entry are indicated by *.

atua*	spirit, god
haka	dance, song accompanying a dance
hine	often the first element in a woman's name
mana*	influence, prestige, power
marae	ceremonial space in front of a house
mauri*	life principle, source of vitality, protector of mana
mere	short, flat striking weapon of greenstone
noa	everyday, without restriction
ngārara	reptile (gecko or tuatara)
ngāruru	Cook's turban shell
pā	fortress
Pākehā	person of European descent
patu	short, flat striking weapon
poupou	upright slab in wall of house
puhi	high-ranking young woman who was cherished and carefully guarded before marriage
rangatira	chief, person of high rank
taiaha	long, two-handed weapon with blade at one end and point at the other
taniwha*	being with special powers that lives, usually, in the sea or inland waters
tapu*	sacred, under religious restriction
tipua:	being with special powers
tohunga*	priest, expert
tūāhu*	shrine
wairua*	soul, spirit
waka	canoe, ship

Index